DARE TO SHINE!

Making positive choices in a negative world

10 Principles to build a great Future

And Discover Your Destiny

A guidebook for the Teenager and Youth

BY

ROSEMARY OKOLO

THE AUTHOR OF SPEAK THE WORD IN THE FACE OF YOUR CIRCUMSTANCES

authorHOUSE®

AuthorHouse™ UK Ltd.
500 Avebury Boulevard
Central Milton Keynes, MK9 2BE
www.authorhouse.co.uk
Phone: 08001974150

First published by AuthorHouse 4/5/2011

ISBN: 978-1-4567-7703-6 (sc)
ISBN: 978-1-4567-7704-3 (e)

DEDICATION

I dedicate this book to my three lovely children: Sophia, Micaiah and Dorothy. And to every teenager and youth who reads this book, with the hope and prayer that they will all utilize these 10 life changing principles in their own lives and make the right choices that will cause them to shine in the midst of a dark world, build a great future and discover their destiny.

ACKNOWLEDGEMENTS

I would like to acknowledge my husband, Charles, I really do appreciate you and always thank God for your life. Thank you for standing with me throughout the course of this book. Thank you for your love, prayers, and words of wisdom, support and encouragement. I couldn't have accomplished this without you. You are truly a precious gift from Heaven. I love you with all my heart.

Sophia, Micaiah and Dorothy, my three lovely children: I thank you for giving me the time and space needed to write this book. Thank you for your patience and understanding. I am so proud of you.

Finally, a big thank you to all who have supported encouraged and challenged me over the years and during the course of this book. I love and appreciate you.

To God be all the glory!

Contents

Introduction

"I call heaven and earth to witness this day against you that I have set before you life and death, the blessings and the curses; therefore choose life that you and your descendants may live." Deuteronomy 30:19

One of the greatest assets we all have as human beings that set us apart from every other living being on earth is the power to make choices; the ability to choose the course of our lives and the kind of life we want to live. It is indeed the greatest power ever bestowed upon mankind. However, we must realise that every choice we make in life always comes with consequences, which may be positive or negative.

The teenage and youth years should be a time to enjoy life, but it is also a very crucial time when you have to decide the direction or path your life will take. The question is will the direction or path you choose ultimately lead you to a life of joy, happiness, a productive, effective life and a life of peace? Or will it lead you into one of fear, pain, depression, unhappiness and a life of failure both now and in the future?

Friend, God has an awesome plan and purpose for every one of you. He has a great destiny for you to fulfil. However, you cannot walk in this destiny if you keep making the wrong choices in life which will ultimately destroy your great future. Do you know that your level of success or failure in life is dependent on the choices you make today? Have you ever thought of the fact that your destiny comes not through chance but through choice? That the decisions of your tomorrow reflect the choices you make today? The power to create a great future for yourself or a life of failure is in your hands, even by the choices you make today.

Dear friend, the choices you make mould your character and ultimately shape your future. What choices are you making daily? Are these choices moulding your character into the image of God and shaping your future in the direction of success, peace and happiness or are your choices moulding your character and future into one of failure, bitterness and turmoil? It has been said that what we think, what we know or what we believe is, in the end, of little consequence. The only consequence is what we do by the choices we have made.

"The freedom of choice is not a formal abstract capacity which one either 'has' or 'has not'; it is rather, a function of a person's character structure. Some people have no freedom to choose the good because their character structure has lost the capacity to act in accordance with the good. Some people have lost the capacity of choosing the evil, precisely because their character structure has lost the craving for evil... The longer we continue to make the wrong decisions, the more our heart hardens; the more often we make the right decisions, the more our heart softens – or better perhaps, become alive" ---- Eric Fromm: The heart of man.

We all make choices everyday and as we get older, we make more choices; these choices become greater which also leads to greater consequences. The purpose of this book, is to get you to understand and have a clearer picture about the choices you make in life and their consequences and the fact that although, as a teenager, youth, young man or woman you are able to make your own choices and choose a course of action, you cannot choose the consequences of your choices. In other words, you have no control of the consequences of the choices you choose to make.

It is also very important to know that the choices you make today, would not only affect you, but it will affect others both now and in the future; and these people it affects may be unable to choose the consequences of your actions. Life they say is hard and unfair. But could it be as a result of the bad choices you have made or that you are making? Could it be that where you are today and some of the things you are struggling with, the hardship you are experiencing, the bitterness in your heart, the pain, continuous failure you are experiencing and life you are living right now is as a result of the choices you have made or the choices that others have made!

"ARISE [from the depression and prostration in which circumstances have kept you. Rise to a new life]! Shine (be radiant with the glory of the Lord), for your light has come, and the glory of the Lord has risen upon you!" Isaiah 60:1

God has called you into a great destiny. He wants you to be the best and have the best in life. He wants you to shine in the midst of a dark world. It is time to Arise and shine friend, for your light has come! It is my prayer that this book will open your eyes to the truth of God's Word. That you will come to understand the power in the choices you make and the fact that every choice comes with a consequence. You are where you are today, because of the choices you made yesterday. This is a guidebook to a great future. Make a difference and DARE TO SHINE!

Rosemary Okolo

Think on these:

It has been said that Destiny is not a matter of chance; but that it is a matter of choice; And that it is not something to be waited for; but something to be achieved. However, the ability to achieve your destiny is dependent on the choices you make today. Make the right choices and discover your destiny!

Principle #1
Your Choices have consequences!

The issue of making right choices is so important today and now, especially in a time and age as these, where a lot of teenagers and the youth, young men and women of all ages are being bombarded with peer pressure to follow the crowd, seeking after fleeting pleasures that are but temporal and will not and cannot bring any lasting happiness to them; making wrong choices that end up damaging their bodies, self worth and ultimately destroying their lives and destiny.

A time and age where teenagers and the youth are suffering and dying from the effects of alcohol, tobacco, drugs and harmful substances to achieve a so called 'high' and engaging in illicit sex which has now become a common thing among them; disobeying the law and damning the consequences. A generation of people who have a laid back attitude toward the Word of God and the things of God, who go to church but have no church in them. This is the time to make right choices!

Life is full of choices

Dear friend, life is full of choices. The minute you wake up in the morning, you have about a thousand choices to make; from whether or not to get out of bed, to how your day would be, what to do, how to do it, where to go etc. First and foremost, I want you to understand this fact that, God created you with a great destiny, and a purpose. You were created for greatness. Friend, the decisions and choices you make today will define your tomorrow. For the choices you make will ultimately determine your destiny. Your choices in life reveal your preferences, your dreams and your aspirations; your choices reveal who you really are and who you will be!

Moses made a choice that changed his life and destiny forever; a choice that not only affected him, but affected the children of Israel. We see in Hebrews 11:25-26, where the Bible says of Moses:

"Choosing rather to suffer affliction with the people of God than to enjoy the passing pleasures of sin, esteeming the reproach of Christ greater riches than the treasures in Egypt; for he looked to the reward."

Friend, do you choose to please your friends rather than pleasing God? Would you rather go with the crowd just because 'everyone is doing it' rather than choose to follow the principles of God's Word? In the above passage, we see that Moses was prepared to please God rather than men. He was ready to forego the pleasures of Egypt and follow after God and the will of God for his life regardless of the circumstances. The Bible says of Moses, that he esteemed the reproach of Christ greater riches than the treasures of Egypt. Moses esteemed the will of God for his life above every other thing, even above the pleasures of being a prince in the house of Pharaoh.

Who are you esteeming above God's Word? What are you esteeming above the will and purpose of God for your life? Moses had a choice and he chose to make the right choice in spite of the circumstances. God wants you to do the same. He wants you to esteem His Word above anything and anyone. The Word of God should be more esteemed than anything else in your life.

What choices are you making right now? You see, Moses was in a situation where he was given an opportunity to live in the Palace and enjoy the wealth and pleasures of Egypt but he chose to throw away his prince hood and suffer as a mere man. He chose rather, to live as a fugitive as it were rather than live as a prince. Moses knew who he was, and chose to allow the will of God for his life to take first place, to take priority. His decision affected not only him, but the whole of the Nation of Israel. Moses delivered them from the bondage and yoke of Egypt and gave them their freedom.

"By faith he took Egypt, not fearing the wrath of the King; for he endured as seeing Him who is invisible. By faith he kept the

Passover and the sprinkling of blood, lest he who destroyed the firstborn should touch them. By faith they passed through the Red Sea as by land, whereas the Egyptians, attempting to do so, were drowned." Hebrew 11:27-29

How many times have you been in situations or found yourself in certain situations that would have seemingly given you an advantage but rather than enjoy that advantage, you chose to do the right thing, choosing to obey God and His Word rather than men or your flesh? Are there certain relationships you need to quit or change and walk away from? Are there old habits that you need to quit? Are there places that you need to quit going to? Make fulfilling your destiny a priority in your life. Choose today to make the right choices!

Suffice to say that to determine if your choices are good, they must be choices that line up with God's Word, with God's will and purpose for your life; choices that will ultimately bring praise and glory to God. Remember, good choices will help you avoid and overcome challenges. Bad choices can and will mess up your life and your future.

Your choices mould you

While here on earth, we all make choices that determine the course, quality and effectiveness of our lives. Some of which are very important and some of which are not. Suffice to say that many of these choices are between good and evil. However, the choices you make, determine to a great extent your happiness or your unhappiness, and you will have to live with the consequences of your choices.

It has been said that you are what you are because of the choices you have made. And that in the long run, you shape your life and you shape yourself. The process never ends until you die. And the choices you make are ultimately your responsibility and no one else's. We all make choices about our job, the friends we hang out with, what to eat, what to wear, what we say, where we go and the list goes on and on. Today, you made the decision to pick up this book to read. Friend, what choices are you making or have you made regarding your future; the call of God upon your life; Your God given gifting; your career; who you would marry? What choices are you making regarding your relationship with God and your destiny? Have you ever thought about the fact that your choices may not only affect you but may also affect others?

The Bible gives numerous examples of decisions with which some people were faced and the result of the choices they made. Like Jonah in the book of Jonah 1:1-14 who made the wrong choice to run away from God's instructions to him, putting the lives of other innocent men at risk almost taking the lives of these men in the ship!

Choices and consequences

Joseph was faced with a lot of challenges see Genesis 39 but he made the decision to remain faithful to God and forgive all who had hurt him one way or the other. Joseph made the right choices each time regardless of the circumstances.

Daniel was also a man who had lots of challenges and pressure upon him. In Daniel 1:5, when the king assigned to them the portion of the kings meat and wine (which would have been offered to the kings gods and idols), Daniel had the choice to enjoy it and say well, 'I had no choice' but Daniel determined in his heart not to partake of it (Daniel 1:8). You see, Daniel had made up his mind long before, when he was in Jerusalem before he and the others were carried away that he would live a life of faithfulness and honour to God. When faced with this situation to defile himself with the king's food, he made the choice not to eat of it, no matter the cost or consequences.

Judas Iscariot made the choice to betray Jesus. He chose to enjoy the pleasures of sin, even the love for money but never got to enjoy that money. You see, there is pleasure in sin, but the pleasure is just for a moment and the consequences are grave. Judas made the wrong choice. Samson chose to play with sin even with his eyes open. He chose to disobey God's instructions to him regarding his call. He chose to satisfy his lustful desires rather than God's will for his life. Samson made the wrong choice.

4

Adam and Eve chose to disobey God and ate of the forbidden fruit. Of the two thieves crucified with Jesus on either side of Him, one chose to mock Him and the other chose to trust Him. One made the right choice and the other made a wrong choice. Lot made the wrong choice which caused him and his family great terrible consequences and loss. His daughters committed incest with him and he lost his wife who turned into a pillar of salt forever. See genesis 13:1-11 Abraham chose to trust and obey God to sacrifice his only son to the Lord. He chose to love God above his son, rather than love his son above God. Abraham made the right choice. Esther the Queen also made the choice to go see the king before she was called by him (which was against the kings law) and was prepared to damn the consequences even if it meant death for her. See Esther 4:1-16

You see, the choices of the ones who trusted and obeyed God and His Son Jesus, and were prepared to sacrifice the pleasures of this life for something greater, who were prepared to sacrifice even their own lives for the sake of others, brought about remarkable results of great joy, peace, honour, promotion, deliverance, protection, increase and the blessings of God upon their lives and families. On the other hand, the choices of the ones who chose to have their own way and do their own thing rather than God's will and purposes for their lives, who could not let go of the pleasures of sin and obey God and making the wrong choices, brought upon themselves consequences that they did not foresee when they made their decisions. Their choices brought upon themselves and families hardship, sorrow, shame, pain and ultimately, death.

What choices are you making?

Friend, what do you love above God? Who are you placing above God and His Word? Is it that boy friend of yours, money, and addiction? Are you making the right choices in life? Remember, there are consequences!

"It is obvious what kind of life develops out of trying to get your own way all the time: repetitive, loveless, cheap sex; a stinking accumulation of mental and emotional garbage; frenzied and joyless grabs for happiness; trinket gods; magic show religion;

paranoid loneliness; cutthroat competition; all consuming, yet never satisfied wants; a brutal temper; an impotence to love or be loved; divided homes and divided lives; small minded and lopsided pursuits; the vicious habit of depersonalizing everyone into a rival; uncontrolled and uncontrollable addictions; ugly parodies of community. I could go on. This isn't the first time I have warned you, you know. If you use your freedom this way, you will not inherit God's Kingdom." Galatians 5:19-21 (the Message)

What choices are you making regarding your everyday life? In your relationships, your habits, and walk with God? Jesus was also faced with choices but He chose to obey the will of God (Matthew 26:53) to die for your sins and mine. Jesus is our ultimate example. When you allow the Holy Spirit to rule in your life, and when you are faced with many choices, it makes it easier to know which way you should go or take. We are always bombarded with choices, as life is often a series of ups and downs, highs and lows, happy and sad experiences. It is the choice you make that can take you closer or further away from your dreams, vision and your destiny!

"My counsel is this: live freely, animated and motivated by God's Spirit. Then you won't feed the compulsions of selfishness. For there is a root of sinful self interest in us that is at odds with a free spirit, just as the free spirit is incompatible with selfishness. These two ways of life are antithetical, so that you cannot live at times one way and at times another way according to how you feel on any given day. Why don't you choose to be led by the Spirit and so escape the erratic compulsions of a law dominated existence?" Galatians 5:16-18 (the Message)

Friend, it may seem tough at first to change from just making any decision to making the right choices in life. You may even face criticism and possible opposition from your friends, colleagues, classmates and your peers just because of your decision to make the right choice; don't give up, stand firm and strong in the confidence of God's Word. Knowing that the choices you make determine your future and your destiny. Making the right choices would sometimes cause you to step out of your comfort zone. Sometimes you may have to stand on your own all by yourself, but guess what? It's worth it! Remain focused on your decisions and trust in the grace of God to see you through. You can do all things that God has called you to do through Christ Jesus!

"I have strength for all things in Christ who empowers me [I am ready for anything and equal to anything through Him who infuses inner strength into me; I am self sufficient in Christ's sufficiency]." Philippians 4:13

"But He said to me, my grace (my favour and loving kindness and mercy) is enough for you [sufficient against any danger and enables you to bear the trouble manfully]; for my strength and power are made perfect (fulfilled and completed) and show themselves most effective in [your] weakness. Therefore, I will all the more gladly glory in my weaknesses and infirmities, that the strength and power of Christ (the Messiah) may rest infirmities, that the strength and power of Christ (the Messiah) may rest (yes, may pitch a tent over and dwell) upon me!" 2 Corinthians 12:9 (the message)

God created us to be a people who are capable of making the right choices. It is never too late to make the right choice. Remember, when you have made your choice, you have no power to choose the consequences. You must therefore base your decisions on the Word of God and not on the World's systems and way of doing things; and certainly not by your emotions. Be determined today to make the right choice. And see your life change for good! Be the difference; make a difference and DARE TO SHINE! Yes, you can.

Remember:

- Making the right choices would sometimes cause you to step out of your comfort zone.

- Jesus was also faced with choices but He chose to obey the will of God (Matthew 26:53) to die for your sins and mine. Jesus is our ultimate example.

- It has been said that you are what you are because of the choices you have made.

- It is also very important to know that the choices you make today, would not only affect you, but it will affect others both now and in the future.

- The Word of God should be more esteemed than anything else in your life.

Think on these:

Friend, the decisions and choices you make today will define your tomorrow. For the choices you make will ultimately determine your destiny.

Your thoughts:

Study Questions

1. Do you now realise that the choices you make have consequences?

What decisions are you making concerning your life; are they right choices?

----

2. Do you know that your choices mould your character? What choices then are you making regarding your walk with God?

----

3. Are your choices based on the Word of God; if not, what are they based on?

----

4. What choices are you making regarding your relationships, habits friends and your future?

Principle #2
Identity - A Winning Attitude!

How do I look? How well am I doing? Am I good enough? Am I intelligent enough? Am I matching up? Am I looking cool? Am I well dressed? Is my hair well made? What do you think about me? We all have asked these questions one time or the other in our lives and we believed that the answer to these questions is to compare ourselves with one another. In other words, we make other people our reference point. Therefore in the long run, our success or failure now depends on the people around us who are the basis of our comparison. This I must say is foolishness.

Sometimes we wish we were someone else, not realising that, that person may actually have wished that they were you. Guess what? They also have their own short fallings and have their own imperfections. The truth is, nothing can and should define who you are. Having a low self esteem is a major challenge for many people in our Society today. This is absolutely true for men, women, teenagers and the youth and in all stages of life. Dare to be you, dare to be proud of who you are and embrace it. Learn to celebrate yourself! You deserve it.

Self esteem

Self esteem is not just having self confidence. This is because, there are a great number of people, celebrities, actors, actresses, singers and professional athletes, who do so well and look confident in front of the camera and on stage but when they are off stage or off the camera and all by themselves, they still have a sense of depression and insecurity, which leads them into having to depend on drugs to keep them fit and confident. That is not self esteem at all. The word 'esteem' is said to be a Latin word that means 'to estimate'. Therefore, self esteem is how you estimate or regard yourself. It is what you think of yourself; it is how you like yourself; self esteem is having a positive belief in yourself and being confident and comfortable with whom you are in spite of where you are or what you have; it is having a good self image based on how you see yourself through God's Word!

A low self esteem is the reverse. It is having a poor self image, not being confident and comfortable with whom you are and who you were created by God to be; not believing in yourself, and thinking everyone else is better than you. Friend, a low self esteem will cause you to think negatively about yourself and cause you to pay attention and believe the criticism others may have of you, and ultimately take away your self confidence. It has been said that having a good self image is the key determinant of your performance and success level in anything you do.

Dear friend, Geneticists say that no one has a duplicate of our genes. Sociologists say that no one has a duplicate of our experiences. Paul said that we all have gifts that differ. Having gifts (faculties, talents, qualities) that differ according to the grace given us...Romans 12:6 where then is the basis for comparison if you are unique? How can you compare the incomparable? The world's system is to compare you with others. That's completely insane and totally wrong.

Not that we [have the audacity to] venture to class or [even to] compare ourselves with some who exalt and furnish testimonials for themselves. However, when they measure themselves with themselves and compare themselves with one another, they are without understanding and behave unwisely. 2 Corinthians 10:12

When you compare yourself with others, you are not wise. One Bible translation says that 'you are foolish'. You will always feel inadequate when you compare yourself with someone else. Do not look at yourself through the worlds mirror such as the media, the model actors and actresses you see on TV, internet, in magazines and movies or some other factors. It's not clear, it's not real and it's definitely not the true image of you or who you should be.

You will never feel good about yourself, love who you are and be stable if your perception about yourself comes from how people see you or what people say about you; In other words, people's opinions about you. Rather look at yourself in the mirror of God's Word and what the Word says about you. Friend, look at you through God's Word. His Word is your mirror, blueprint, standard and your final reference point. God's Word is our final authority. Period!

What value have you placed on yourself?

What opinion do you have of yourself? What value have you placed on yourself? It has been said that if you place a small value on yourself, you can be sure that the world will not raise your price. Is the value you have of yourself based on what you do, and your job? How much you earn? Where you live or how big your house is? Is it based on who you know? Who your parents are? Who your husband or wife is? The things you have? What you have accomplished? Is it based on your looks?

The truth is that, if the value you place on yourself is based on all of these things, you will eventually realise that you have no true value of yourself and do not really know who you truly are and have based your value on a wrong foundation. For all of these things are temporal and therefore subject to change. But rather place or base your value on the foundation of God's Word. For everything else will change and fail, but God's Word will never change or fail and it abides forever, for God abides forever!

In the beginning [before all time] was the Word (Christ), and the Word was with God, and the Word was God Himself. John 1:1

Child of God, you have great value because you were created by God. You are of great value and precious in His sight. Do not disqualify yourself. You are so very significant and loved in the sight of God that He sent His Son Jesus to die for you. Friend, if you were the only human on earth, Jesus would still have died for you. Please don't look down at yourself. Lift your head up high and square up your shoulders and know that you are so important in the awesome plan of God in this generation. God needs you! It is very important for you to always have a healthy sense of self worth. Love yourself and who God has created you to be. To be you! It's okay to be you and yes it's okay to be different. Notice I said different, not weird.

Most young men and women, youth and especially teenagers, struggle with their self worth at some point in their lives, even though they may look confident on the outside. For some it was caused due to a divorce by both parents who made them feel it was their fault. For some, the divorce caused them to feel a sense of shame before their peers; for others it may be a lack of education, failure in education, a disability, living in abject poverty, negative words spoken into their lives especially from someone very close to them, neglect, physical, or domestic abuse, and even sexual abuse, being told that you were born out of a mistake and the list goes on.

Dear friend, I know all of these hurts and can be so discouraging and demoralising. However, you don't have to live that way. Don't ever allow people's opinion of you to take the better part of your life. Don't even allow their views and opinion of you to become your reality. You were never a mistake. The Word of God says that God knew you ever before you were formed in your mother's womb, and has a plan and a purpose for you, that only you can accomplish. He has put some natural and special endowment and ability in you to do something great for His kingdom. But you have got to believe God's Word and believe in yourself and in your ability. Love yourself! Be proud of you. Choose to make that choice today.

Do not allow anything, anyone or any circumstance to define who you are. It doesn't matter what you are going through right now or what your situation looks like. Never allow your circumstances dominate you or define you. Remember, you are who God says you are regardless of your circumstances which are subject to change anyway.

You are special and unique

I remember many years ago, when I was a teenager (an ignorant one I must say), I didn't like the way I looked. I always used to wish back then that I was taller, better looking, with a small thin straight nose, beautiful legs, a small waist and so on and so forth. And when I saw others with those features, i always thought to myself that, they were better than me. I thought they were just 'it.'

I compared myself with other people and other teenage girls I knew or had seen. I compared myself with the actresses on TV, and in a magazine; I tried to dress like them, and talk like them hoping it would make me feel better about myself and be appreciated and liked. But it was quite hard to keep up with all of that and it eventually caused me not to appreciate myself and who I was. I felt that I wasn't good enough and therefore not good enough to have the best or be the best in life. I always thought I only deserved second best. I really didn't like who I was and this had such a negative effect on me and made me unable to communicate effectively with people. I had such a low self esteem, felt inferior and lacked confidence in myself. The devil is a liar!

Then one day, I heard a message preached in church on inferiority complex that changed my life forever! Oh thank God for that day and for that message! I went back home, searched the Word and realised that God didn't want me to feel that way about myself and that He truly loved me just the way I was and had put so much potential and gifting in me to use for His Glory. Wow, I saw in God's Word that I was significant in God's plan, that He wants me to have the best in life and be the best in life, that He had created me for a purpose, that I am His master piece, that I have a great destiny, that He loves me the same way He loves His Son Jesus. Friend, my life has never been the same again ever since that day. I know better now and I am going to pursue His will and purpose for my life and be the best that He has called me to be and fulfil all that God has called me to do here on earth and fulfil my destiny! I will not allow anything or anyone stop me. You can choose to make that decision too.

See yourself the way God sees you

God loves you so very much. He has put greatness on the inside of you. He wants you to be the best that you can be. To wish that you are somebody else is to waste the person that you are. No one can ever do a better job of being you than you. Someone once said that it's not who you are that holds you back, but it's who you think you are not. Nobody can make you feel inferior without your consent.

Jeremiah 29:11 says that God's thoughts and plans for you are thoughts and plans for welfare and peace and not for evil, to give you hope in your final outcome. See Jeremiah 1:5

Friend, God knew you even before you were born into this world and He had chosen and approved of you. God loves you and accepts you the very way that you are! Whether tall, short, fat, thin, black, white, Caribbean, Asian, regardless of how you feel or think you look. You are beautiful in His eyes and that's all that matters. He knew you before the world was created. You are His and He cares about you. You belong to Him. You do not own yourself. Romans 1:6 God bought you with a costly price.

1 Corinthians 6:20 says, you were bought with a price [purchased with a preciousness and paid for, made His own]. So then, honour God and bring glory to Him in your body.

You were born into the world because it was His good pleasure. Don't look down at yourself. You are special. You were created in the image of God, after His likeness. Do not think of yourself as a failure. You are not a failure, you are a success! The Bible says that you are the head and not the tail, you are above only and not beneath, you were created for signs and wonders, you are absolutely precious in God's sight, you are the light of the world, you are an adequate competent minister of His Word. You are His workmanship, created in Christ Jesus for good works, you have a great destiny and neither man nor the devil can stop it. Only you can stop it. Isn't that just awesome!

Growing up, you may have received messages that affected and damaged your self- esteem. You may have been called names; you may have been told that you will never amount to anything good in life, that you will be a failure that no man would ever look at you twice not to talk of proposing marriage to you. You may have been told that no woman would love you, that you were too dull to ever graduate from secondary school or the University that you will end up a drunk like your father who died with nothing to his name.

You may have been told that you will die having nothing good to your name too. Friend, you may have been told so many negative things not mentioned here and as a result, you gradually began to believe these words and began to see yourself that way, lost connection with your abilities, strengths and gifting, as you now try to live up to other people's expectations rather than yours. For some of you, this has meant getting into a career, a relationship, a job, living a lifestyle of your parents choosing or someone else instead of deciding for yourself. Pleasing others in hopes of being accepted, and losing your self- worth. It's not worth it friend! It's not worth it at all. Quit trying to live other people's dreams and lives and start living yours. However, you must renew your mind to this truth.

Change your way of thinking

It has been said that, the mental aspect of our lives is more important than our physical presence. And that all we are and all we have the potential to become is nothing more than the product of our thoughts. Proverbs 23:7 says for as he thinks in his heart, so is he... if you think negatively, real soon and you will begin to act in that same direction – negatively. Do you realise that you are what you think? If you see yourself as no good, that's exactly what you will become. Start thinking right friend. Come out of that negative way of thinking and seeing yourself and begin to see yourself as God sees you!

Begin to say positive things about yourself even when you don't see it. God has given you the ability to succeed in life and it is within you. Make up your mind today to stop listening to discouraging words and people's negative opinions about you. Believe in yourself for God believes in you. Nobody can stop you from succeeding, but you. You are your limitation. Get rid of your limitations! If God be for you, who can be against you?

Genesis 12:1-4 says now [in Haran] the Lord said to Abram, go for yourself [for your advantage] away from your country, from your relatives and your father's house, to the land that I will show you. And I will make of you a great nation, and I will bless you [with abundant increase of favours] and make your name famous and distinguished, and you will be a blessing [dispensing good to

others]. And I will bless those who bless you [who confer prosperity or happiness upon you] and curse him who curses or uses insolent language toward you; in you will all the families and kindred of the earth be blessed [and by you they will bless themselves]. So Abram departed, as the Lord had directed him...

God wants you to come out from amongst the people who speak negative things into your life, people who look down on you and think little of you; from people who compare themselves with you, who make you feel inferior when you are amongst them, from the traditions of your fathers and mothers and their ways of living and thinking, from your past experiences, come out from those bad habits that seem to be holding you down, that way of life that is contrary to God's way of living, and most of all, God wants you to also come out of that mind set of yours, from those thoughts that are holding you bound, come out of your way of thinking.

That mentality that is not in line with God's Word and contrary to His will and purpose for your life. Friend, you must depart like Abram did. God wants you to rise to your full potential; He wants you to arise to your covenant rights in Him. The greater one and His anointing lives on the inside of you; Raise your head up high and walk with confidence in that knowledge. Change the negative information you have been receiving into your mind to positive ones. Begin today to read the Bible daily and re programme your mind and your thoughts with the Word of God.

Isaiah 60:1 says Arise, [from the depression and prostration in which circumstances have kept you – rise to a new life]! Shine (be radiant with the glory of the Lord has risen upon you!

Forget the past and look forward

No, dear brothers and sisters, I have not achieved it, but I focus on this one thing: forgetting the past and looking forward to what lies ahead, I press on to reach the end of the race and receive the heavenly prize for which God, through Christ Jesus, is calling us. Philippians 3:13-14 (NLT)

Paul understood what it meant to forget the past. You all know his story. He had a terrible past; he had some very bad experiences too. However, he chose to forget the past. We all have some short comings, but instead of focussing on those short comings, make the choice like Paul did to forget and look forward to what lies ahead. "Oh but you don't know what I have been through... you don't know what people have said about me, the names they called me, you don't know what I've done". Friend, stop looking back at your past experiences and failures. Do not allow a low self esteem keep you bound. There is no past in your future. If you do not let go of your past, you will be stuck there and not move forward in life. It would hold you back from embracing the awesome future God has for you.

This is the day that the Lord has made, and we shall rejoice and be glad in it. Make the choice today; refuse to allow feelings of inferiority, a low self esteem and guilt into your life. A low self esteem will stop you from getting the best in life. It will cripple you and stop you from fulfilling your destiny in God. It's a burden that can destroy you and the purpose of God in your life. Do not be concerned about what people think about you neither consider their opinions. Be more concerned with what God says and thinks about you. Consider only His Word! God loves you friend!

Romans 5:8 says, but God shows and clearly proves His [own] love for us by the fact that while we were still sinners, Christ (the Messiah, the Anointed One) died for us.

Forget the former things; do not dwell on the past. Isaiah 43:18 (NIV)

You may not be able to change your past but you can choose today, to change your future! Remember, it's not what people think or say about you that matters, it's what you think and say about yourself that matters. Raise your head up child of God and love YOU! Dare to be different. Only you can make that choice.

"Our deepest fear is not that we are inadequate. Our deepest fear is that we are powerful beyond measure. It is our light, not our darkness that most frightens us. We ask ourselves, who am I to be brilliant, gorgeous, talented, and fabulous? Actually, who are you not to be? You are a child of God. Your playing small does not serve the world. There is nothing enlightened about shrinking so that other people won't feel insecure around you. We are all meant to shine, as children do. We were born to make manifest the glory of God that is within us. It is not just in some of us; it is in everyone. And as we let our own light shine, we unconsciously give other people permission to do the same. As we are liberated from our own fear, our presence automatically liberates others". - Marianne Williamson, *A Return to Love: Reflections on the Principles of "A Course in Miracles,"* 1992

No one of us is worth more or less than another. That's why you should never compare yourself with someone else, be it your brother, sister, cousin, friend or neighbour. Do not allow a low self esteem to strip you off of your God given potential, unique gifting and talents. Having a good self worth or self esteem is a choice you would have to make every day. The enemy always does things to make us hurt but the devil is a liar! Refuse his plans for your life. Maybe you don't feel confident right now, but you can be confident and you will be. It doesn't matter what you are going through right now, do not allow your circumstances define you. Your beginning may be small but your end shall greatly increase!

Start today to begin to build a good healthy self worth by the renewing of your mind through the Word of God. Our life is transformed by the renewing of our minds. It may not just happen in a day but keep at it, don't give up and see what God would do with your life. Until you find your purpose in God and let go of everything that is holding you down, and seek after God and His gifting in your life, you will continue to be like a dog chasing after its own tail. Make the choice to spend quality time studying the Word of God daily. Remember, you are of great significance in the sight of God. He created you for greatness. Never ever forget that!

Oh yes, you shaped me first inside, and then out; you formed me in my mother's womb. I thank you, High God – you're breathtaking! Body and soul, I am marvellously made! I worship in adoration – what a creation! You know me inside and out, you know every

bone in my body; you know exactly how I was made, bit by bit, how I was sculpted from nothing into something. Like an open book, you watched me grow from conception to birth; all the stages of my life were spread out before you, the days of my life all prepared before I'd even lived one day. Psalm 139:13-16 (the Message Bible)

Someone once said that "a man's mind may be likened to a garden, which may be intelligently cultivated or allowed to run wild; but whether cultivated or neglected, it must and will bring forth. If no useful seeds are put into it, then an abundance of useless weed seeds will fall therein and will continue to produce their kind."

Friend, what seeds are you allowing or sowing into your heart and mind? Is it seeds of God's Word or the opinions of people? Plant the seed of God's Word into your heart and mind today. God loves you and believes in you. Make the choice today to begin to believe in you. Remember, there is greatness on the inside of you. Dare to be different, make a difference and DARE TO SHINE!

Remember:

- You were born into the world because it was His good pleasure. Don't look down at yourself. You are special.

- Do not allow anything, anyone or any circumstance to define who you are.

- You are so very significant and precious in the sight of God that He sent His Son Jesus to die for you.

- A low self esteem will stop you from getting the best in life. It will cripple you. It's a burden that can destroy you and the purpose of God in your life.

- Remember, there is greatness on the inside of you and only you can bring it out. Take the lid off your life and break the barriers of a low self esteem!

Think on these:

You will never feel good about yourself and be stable if your perception about yourself comes from how people see you. Rather look at yourself in the mirror of God's Word and what the Word says about you.

Your thoughts:

Study Questions

1. How do you see yourself?

----

2. What does God's Word say about you?

----

3. Whose opinions should matter more to you and why?

----

4. What are your strengths and what are you doing about them?

----

5. What does the Word say about changing the way you think?

Principle #3
Integrity – Your Finest Asset!

We are living in a generation that is getting darker and darker each passing day; A world where immorality, dishonesty, bribery and corruption, deception and negative competition with one another is considered as being okay and the norm; A society where teenagers, youth, young men and women have learnt how to game the system, fudge numbers and are losing their values, principles and faith and living a life of compromise without any feeling of shame or concern. An age that is becoming more challenging to live holy and in integrity.

We are living in an age and generation where the word called integrity is becoming a rare commodity and fast fading away. Sadly, this same attitude and spirit of compromise and a lack of integrity has crept into the Church today. Where, our teenagers and youth have a lackadaisical attitude towards truth, God's Word, standards and His ways of doing things; Where men and women in positions of authority, leaders in some churches cannot be trusted, relied upon; They tell you to do as they 'say', and not as they 'do'; People who are not transparent and lack the strength of character – integrity.

Friend, being a Christian is more than just saying you are one, or having faith in God's Word, it's more than just going to church every now and then and acting so sanctimonious, it's more than just hanging around Christian folks and hearing the Word of God. It is more than sticking a Christian postal on your door. Let me burst your bubble, it's more than studying the Word and speaking in tongues. Being a Christian is having a personal relationship with Jesus and being a doer of His Word and not just a hearer of it. It is talking the talk and walking the walk. It is being a person of integrity!

But be doers of the Word [obey the message], and not merely listeners to it, betraying yourselves [into deception by reasoning contrary to the Truth]. James 1:22

Matthew 22:16 the message says, "Teacher, we know you have integrity, teach the way of God accurately, are indifferent to popular opinion, and don't pander to your students..."

Can we take your word to the Bank?

Can others say the same thing about you? Can people say of you that, you are a person of your word, that you say what you do and do what you say? A young girl once said:

"My mum always objects to my living with my boyfriend, she says it's not right for me to do so, yet she spends weekends with her new boyfriend. What's the difference then?"

Friend, do you know that consistently living a life of integrity has everything to do with how your life will turn out to be? If you go to church every now and then, you talk right and look right in front of people, and say the right things but live differently back home, at school, in your place of work you are only deceiving yourself and making life harder and tougher for you? Do you know that when you continue to live this way, yielding to sin, you could become so entangled in it that you may no longer have the will to repent? Please read Hebrews 6:4-9

Proverbs 12:2 the message says, a good person basks in the delight of God, and he wants nothing to do with devious schemers. God cannot lie, He cannot be bribed, His yes is always yes and His no always no. James 5:12 says, But above all [things], my brethren, do not swear, either by heaven or by earth or by any other oath; but let your yes be [a simple] yes, and your no, be [a simple] no, so that you may not sin and fall under condemnation.

God is truth and as His child, you are to be like Him. You are His ambassador. You are Christ's bill boards, to show Christ to the world. Your life is your witness. Action speaks louder than words. Are you demonstrating to the world the character, power and love of God? What words are you constantly speaking out of your mouth? Does it line up with God's Word? Walk your talk. But louder is the one who walks in integrity. God demands integrity from you, in your actions, words and lifestyle. God is integrity. Suffice to say that, Integrity is not a one off thing! Be consistent.

What then is integrity?

The Webster's dictionary defined integrity as 'the quality or state of being complete or undivided or incorruptible'. It has been defined as being true to who you really are; who you are when no one is looking regardless of the circumstances.

"Reuben Gonzales was in the final match of a pro racquetball tournament. In the 4th and final game, at match point, Gonzales made a "super kill" shot into the front wall to win the game. The referee called it good. Two linesmen affirmed that the shot was in. But Gonzales, after a moment's hesitation, turned around, shook his opponent's hand, and declared that his shot had hit the floor first. As a result, he lost the match and walked off the court. Everybody was stunned. They couldn't believe that a player with everything officially in his favour, with victory at hand, disqualified himself at match point and lost!

When asked why he did it, Reuben said "It was the only thing that I could do to maintain my integrity. I could always win another match, but I could never regain my lost integrity."

Dear friend, integrity comes down to the issue of character not just words. God demands that not only do you do the right thing but also with the right heart. What you are on the inside should match what you are on the outside. In other words, there must be consistency between what is inside with what is outside. A person of integrity is consistent. They do what they say, their no is no, they can be predicted and are always consistent. They are not double minded, no duplicity of attitudes and actions.

God is consistent. Paul said in 1Timothy 3:7 that a person must have good reputation and be well thought of by those outside [the church], lest he becomes involved in slander and incur reproach and fall into the devil's trap. Are you a person of integrity? This is a quality you as a Christian should aspire for. You ought to be above reproach in every area of your life. You are the light of the world and immediately you declare that you are a Christian, the world begins to watch you. The life you live is what will be a witness to them whether being a Christian is good or bad and whether you are a Christian or just acting out!

"There was a newspaper story years ago about a man in Long Beach who went into a KFC to get some chicken for himself and the young lady with him. She waited in the car while he went in, to pick up the chicken. Inadvertently, the manager of the store handed the guy the box in which he had placed the financial proceeds of the day instead of the box of chicken. You see, he was going to make a deposit and had camouflaged it by putting the money in a fried chicken box.

The fellow took his box, went back to the car, and the two of them drove away. When they got to the park and opened the box, they discovered they had a box full of money. Now that was a very vulnerable moment for the average individual. However, realizing the mistake, he got back into the car and returned to the place and gave the money back to the manager. Well, the manager was elated! He was so pleased that he told the young man, "stick around, I want to call the newspaper and have them take your picture. You're the most honest guy in town.

"Oh, no, don't do that! Said the fellow; "Why not?" asked the manager. "Well," he said, "you see, I 'm married, and the woman I'm with is not my wife."

You see, he had not really thought about the consequences of his actions. He was trying to do something right, but was also doing something wrong. How many times have you found yourself in such a situation? Doing something similar or even different from this, but where you had to compromise your faith even though you knew better not to. You see, you will have no impact in the world if your life contradicts your message.

How many times have you said okay to something you knew was wrong? Are there situations in your life that you think you have no choice but to lie? And bend the truth because of someone else?

Rather, let our lives lovingly express truth [in all things, speaking truly, dealing truly, and living truly]. Enfolded in love, let us grow up in every way and in all things into Him, who is the head, [even] Christ (the Messiah, the anointed one). Ephesians 4:15

Are you a person of integrity?

Friend, integrity does not blow in the wind or change with the weather. Integrity is constant. It is making an absolute decision not to compromise. It is doing the right thing because it is right, knowing that nobody is going to know whether you did it or not! Integrity will bring stability into your life, regardless of the pressures and challenges around you. Integrity will preserve you. Psalms 25:21 says let integrity and uprightness preserve me. Integrity will protect you. Proverbs 2:7 says He hides away sound and godly wisdom and stores it for the righteous (those who are upright and in right standing with Him); He is a shield to those who walk uprightly and in integrity.

The Bible says of integrity that, the man of integrity walks securely, but he who takes crooked paths will be found out. Proverbs 10:9. The integrity of the upright guides them, but the unfaithful are destroyed by their duplicity. Proverbs 11:3 (NIV)

It has been said that the measure of a man's real character is what he would do if he knew he never would be found out. In other words, integrity means that our private and public life is one before God; to stand before God and man without a guilty conscience.

It's like the story that was said of a man who sent a letter to the internal revenue service. He said, "I cheated on my income taxes, and felt so bad that I couldn't sleep. Enclosed find a cheque for $150 and if I still can't sleep, I'll send the rest of what I owe."

I 'm sure a lot of you can relate to this man. You know it's best to be completely honest, not half way honest. In fact, you want to, but you kind of find it easier to be dishonest. You compromise your values so that a little bit of lying doesn't really bother your conscience. You know you should tithe off 10% of your income, but you don't. Worse still you do tithe, but not the whole 10% you keep a bit of it because, you think no one would know anyway. Friend, half truth is a lie! Partial obedience is disobedience. Integrity means no cutting corners. I read this funny and interesting story and it goes like this:

God is watching you

"A burglar broke into a house one night, and as he began to look around, he heard a strange voice say, "Jesus is watching you," He froze in his tracks and said, "who said that?" No reply. "Must be my conscience," he thought to himself sarcastically. He took a step and heard it again, "Jesus is watching you." "Who said that?" he asked again. "Joshua", was the reply. The burglar turned his flashing light toward the voice and saw a parrot sitting in its cage! Greatly relieved, he laughed and said, "Who would name a parrot Joshua?" the parrot said, "same person who named our pit bull Jesus." (You can make a conclusion of what happened next)

"Mark well that God doesn't miss a move you make; He's aware of every step you take. The shadow of your sin will overtake you; you'll find yourself stumbling all over yourself in the dark. Death is the reward of an undisciplined life; your foolish decisions trap you in a dead end." Proverbs 5:21-23 (the message)

Do you know friend that God is watching you too, even though you cannot see Him? He knows what you do in secret and in the open, He knows your thoughts, what you say, where you go, He knows you better than anyone, and that includes you. He knows everything about you, He sees everything you do and He does care about you. However, He wants you to take your life seriously and do what His Word says, to walk in integrity.

God is concerned about both the little things we do as much as He is concerned about the big things. Little things as going for your lecture at the right time and not missing it, studying properly for your exams, not making unnecessary excuses, being lazy, prioritising your work and time, procrastinating, not telling little 'white lies,' paying for your

TV license if you are using a TV, keeping to your commitments at work, your department in church and your educational establishments, Keeping yourself pure in your relationships, being obedient to your parents and the list goes on and on. You cannot expect to see the manifestations of God's goodness and enjoy His blessings, while living a dishonest lifestyle, and a life of disobedience.

The society and world we live in today make it very challenging to live a life of integrity. People let us down in one way or the other time and time again and again. This is because; there is always a discrepancy between what they claim to believe and how they actually live. But God will never change! He will never ever let you down. His promises are as good as His unchanging character. He is the same yesterday, today, tomorrow and forever.

He is calling you and me to give priority to integrity. He has called you and me to live with them, (the world) but not like them. If you are to be the difference and make a difference in the world as God intends you to be, then you must live a life of integrity. Integrity stands by principles, no matter what the consequences. It is therefore your responsibility to do what the Word says and not what the crowd is saying. Walk away from peer pressure! Make the choice today to live a life of integrity. Remember, His grace is sufficient for you.

Philippians 2:15 says that you may show yourselves to be blameless and guileless, innocent and uncontaminated, children of God without blemish (faultless, unrebukable) in the midst of a crooked and wicked generation [spiritually perverted and perverse], among whom you are seen as bright lights (stars or beacons shinning out clearly) in the [dark] world.

Can you be trusted to be in the place and with the people you have told your parents you will be with? Can you be trusted with the secret of your friend? Can you be trusted with money? Can God trust you? Someone defined integrity as 'wholeness of character, an uncompromising adherence to a code of values, and consistency of word and deed based squarely on the word of God'. This is so true! You see, you can only get your values from God's Word or from the World. Getting your values from the world will cause you pain, frustration and ultimately failure in life!

Integrity requires you to be a student of the Word and apply these to your life. James 1:22-24 from the message Bible says, don't fool yourself into thinking that you are a listener when you are anything but, letting the Word go in one ear and out the other. Act on what you hear! Those who hear and don't act are like those who glance in the mirror, walk away, and two minutes later have no idea who they are, what they look like.

The world is watching you

If you say that you are a Christian but you do not follow the Word of God, you are a liar and a hypocrite. If there is any one group of people that Jesus couldn't stand, it was hypocrites! The Pharisees of Jesus' times were a religious and political party that insisted on very strict observance of Biblical laws on tithing, ritual purity and other matters. At the same time, many of the Pharisees forgot the true spirit and intent of the law and became self indulgent, self righteous, snobbish and greedy. Jesus said of them in Matthew 23:27-28,

"Woe to you, scribes and Pharisees, pretenders (hypocrites)! For you are like tombs that have been whitewashed, which look beautiful on the outside but inside are full of dead men's bones and everything impure. Just so, you also outwardly seem to people to be just and upright but inside you are full of pretence and lawlessness and iniquity".

Samuel was an example of a man of integrity. The Bible says in 1 Samuel 12:3-4 that Israel had a very high regard for him because of his integrity.

"Here I am; testify against me before the Lord and Saul His anointed. Whose ox or donkey have I taken? Or whom have I defrauded or oppressed? Or from whose hand have I received any bribe to blind my eyes? Tell me and I will restore it to you. And they said, you have not defrauded us or oppressed us or taken anything from any man's hand."

Dear friend, if someone were to say a few words about you, would integrity be one of them? Integrity will earn you respect regardless of your age, gender, education or experience. To succeed in whatever you do, you must be a person of integrity.

"After his Sunday messages, the pastor of a church in London got on the trolley Monday morning to return to his study downtown. He paid his fare, and the trolley driver gave him too much change. The pastor sat down and fumbled the change and looked it over, counted it eight times or ten times. And, you know the rationalization, "it's wonderful how God provides." He realised he was tight that week and this was just about what he would need to break even, at least enough for his lunch. He wrestled with himself all the way down that old trolley trail that led to his office. Finally, he came to the stop and got up, and he couldn't live with himself. He walked up to the trolley driver, and said, "Here, you gave me too much change. You made a mistake." The driver said, "No, it was no mistake. You see, I was in your church last night when you spoke on honesty, and I thought I would put you to the test."

Dear reader, do you pass the test each day you are at work, school, with your friends, associates, work colleagues, classmates, business partners, when unbelievers put you to the test because you claim to be a Christian? Can you be trusted with your word? Can you be trusted with money? Can you be trusted with your company's cheque book? Can you be trusted with your girl friend or fiancée when you are all alone by yourself? Can you be trusted with another man's property?

What movies do you watch when no one is around you? What magazines do you read when you are all by yourself? Do you mean what you say, and say what you really mean? Do you keep to your appointments? Do you do what you are asked to do properly? Are you buying stuff you can't afford just to please your friends and peers? Are you a man, woman, boy or girl of your word? Can somebody say of you that, of a truth, your word is your bond? Can you be relied upon? Can God rely on you? Are you a person of integrity?

With integrity, you would have no need to rationalize anything. There would be no need to lie to yourself or others. Integrity causes you to be consistent, no matter the situation. Integrity defines your identity. Could you be undermining your integrity because you are associating with the wrong people? Never ever under estimate your need for integrity. Stay faithful to God. Your ministry success will depend on it. When you live a life of integrity, the opportunities for evangelism and ministry surface; and when you don't, they are taken away.

Dare to be different

Joseph was a man of great integrity; A man who refused to compromise even when it would have been easy to do so. He refused to compromise his standards. He was a man who passed every test and trial that was thrown at him.

Genesis 39:7-9 says then after a time his masters wife cast her eyes upon Joseph and she said to him, lie with me. But he refused and said to his master's wife, see here, with me in the house my master has concern about nothing; he has put all that he has in my care… for you are his wife. How then can I do this great evil and sin against God?

Friend, you see, you cannot have integrity with people without having it with God first. To have integrity with God, you must be willing to put Him first in everything you do no matter the situation or consequences. Matthew 6:33 says but seek (aim at and strive after) first His kingdom and His righteousness (His way of doing and being right), and then all these things taken together will be given you besides. Integrity is what will enable you to reap all of the benefits God promised you in His Word. Integrity will unlock the flow of God's blessings upon your life as promised in His Word. You see, integrity is a very important part of your walk with God. So it was in the life of Joseph. His integrity made a way for him. Genesis 41:38-41 says:

"And Pharaoh said to his servant, can we find this man's equal, a man in whom is the spirit of God? And Pharaoh said to Joseph,

forasmuch as [your] God has shown you all this, there is nobody as intelligent and discreet and understanding and wise as you are. You shall have charge over my house and all my people shall be governed according to your word [with reverence, submission, and obedience]..... See, I have set you over all the land of Egypt."

Daniel is another example of someone who lived a life of integrity even in the midst of mounting pressures and challenges, and God blessed him tremendously. His integrity was what distinguished him among his peers and put him in the place of power and authority above them and caused him to stand before great kings. His integrity brought prosperity, peace blessings and confidence to him.

"Then this Daniel was distinguished above the presidents and the satraps because an excellent spirit was in him, and the king thought to set him over the whole realm. Then the presidents and satraps sought to find occasion [to bring accusation] against Daniel concerning the kingdom, but they could find no occasion or fault, for he was faithful, nor was there any error or fault found in him." Daniel 6:3-4

Have you ever thought, or has it ever crossed your mind why all the wise men, the magicians, the soothsayers, the chaldeans, and the astrologers were unable to translate the words, especially when Daniel's prescribed education in languages was the same as their own and yet he had no difficulty translating it?

It is my submission that all the wise men who were present there probably could recognise the four inscribed words, but could not have an understanding, and revelation of its interpretation, because, only the uncompromising man of God, who knew God through daily fellowship and communion with Him, who was so committed and dedicated to Him, that God could speak to him and through him – only such a man could tell what the words really meant. Daniel was that man. A man of integrity, who knew God, loved God and lived a daily life of fellowship and communion with God. A man whom God could speak to and speak through, a man whom God could depend on!

You cannot do it alone!

I have strength for all things in Christ who empowers me [I am ready for anything and equal to anything through Him who infuses inner strength into me; I am self sufficient in Christ's sufficiency]. Philippians 4:13

Dear friend, you cannot be a person of integrity without God. For without God, integrity is not maintainable. It can only be possible in Christ Jesus. You must have a relationship with God, to walk in integrity.

Psalm 41:12 says "And as for me, you have upheld me in my integrity and set me in your presence."

Are you too busy to spend time with God? Are you too busy to spend time in prayer and the Word? It's not enough to say that you are a Christian, but not having fellowship with God. Becoming a person of integrity is a lifelong process, but it is worth it. Integrity is not something you are born with. Rather it is something you learn and develop over time. And it comes from the daily practice of doing what is right before God and man whether or not somebody is watching you or not. Being obedient to God's Word! However, if you don't make a deliberate plan to be a person of integrity, it will never ever happen. But just because you desire to be a person of integrity, doesn't mean that it would happen overnight. You have to work and walk it!

Friend, being a person of integrity is a choice you would have to make for yourself. Remember, every choice we make, has its consequences which could be either good or bad. Choose today to begin to live a life of integrity.

"In [this] freedom Christ has mad us free [and completely liberated us]; stand fast then, and do not be hampered and held ensnared and submit again to a yoke of slavery [which you have once put off]." Galatians 5:1

If you want to have lasting success in your career, business, relationships, work place, ministry, marriage, and in every area of your life as a teenager, youth, young man or woman, I dare you to make that choice today to a person of integrity. Dare to be trust worthy, honest and reliable no matter the circumstances, no matter the challenges, no matter the consequences. With integrity comes that passion to fulfil purpose. You can achieve it, there is greatness in you. For you were created for greatness. Be the difference; make a difference and DARE TO SHINE!

Remember:

- Integrity will unlock the flow of God's blessings upon your life as promised in His Word.
- If you say that you are a Christian but you do not follow the Word of God, you are a liar and a hypocrite.
- Integrity will earn you respect regardless of your age, gender, education or experience.
- When you live a life of integrity, the opportunities for evangelism and ministry surface; and when you don't, they are taken away.
- It is making an absolute decision not to compromise.

Think on these:

Integrity is said to be wholeness of character, an uncompromising adherence to a code of values, and consistency of word and deed based squarely on the Word of God!

Your thought:

Study Questions

1. What do you understand by the word integrity?

----

2. What does the Bible say about integrity?

----

3. Are you a person of integrity?

----

4. Do you easily give in to pressure from friends just to please them?

----

5. What are those areas in your life that lack integrity?

Principle #4
Friendship – Who are you yoked with!

Someone once said that your companions are like the buttons on an elevator. They will either take you up or they will take you down. It has also been proven that you become the combined average of the five people you hang around the most. That the people you spend your time with determine what conversations dominate your attention, and what observations, attitudes and opinions you repetitively are introduced to. Who you are around can tell me where you are going. A lot of people and especially teenagers are not yet aware of how important this area of choice is and this is the reason for this book. The more knowledge and understanding you have about it, the better you are able to make the right choices about your friendship.

Dear friend, the choice of friends you choose to spend your time with is so vital to who you become and what you become in life. Your friends have a heavy influence in your life whether you know it or not.

Proverbs 12:26 says, the [inconsistently] righteous man is a guide to his neighbour, but the way of the wicked causes others to go astray.

The NIV says a righteous man is cautious in friendship. Friends can help you fulfil your dreams and your God given destiny or discourage you and cause you to give up and never accomplish it.

Do you really know your friends?

I read a story that goes like these: "A Scorpion, being a very poor swimmer, once asked a turtle to carry him on his back across a river. 'Are you mad?' exclaimed the turtle. 'You'll sting me while

I'm swimming and I'll drown.' The Scorpion laughed as he replied, 'my dear turtle, if I was to sting you, you would drown and I would go down with you. Now, what would be the point of that? I won't sting you. It would mean my own death! The turtle thought about the logic of his argument for a few moments and then said, 'you are right. Hop on!' The Scorpion climbed aboard and halfway across the river, he gave the turtle a mighty sting. As the turtle began to sink to the bottom of the river with the scorpion on its back, it moaned in dismay, 'After your promise, you stung me! Why did you do that? Now, we're both doomed.' The drowning scorpion sadly replied, "I couldn't help it. It's my nature to sting."

There is a profound lesson that I want you to learn from this story and that lesson is the fact that you have to study and observe the character of a person before you make them a friend. For the stage on which their character plays is going to be your life. Dear friend, there are two categories of people that exists in the world we live in.

The believers who have a relationship with Jesus (born again Christians) and unbelievers who do not believe God and refuse to accept Jesus Christ as Lord and Saviour of their lives (they have no relationship with God). The Bible clearly states that these two categories are in opposite terms with one another in terms of our belief system. They live by the world's standards and we live by the Word standards (The Bible) and it is from this perspective that we must make the choice of the kind of friendship we can truly have with unbelievers.

1 Corinthians 15:33 says, Do not be so deceived and misled! Evil companionships (communion, associations) corrupt and deprave good manners and morals and character.

What is evil? Anything that opposes God's Word is evil. Not just the evil horror movies you watch or can't watch. Dear friend, if you become deeply involved with unbelievers, notice I said deeply involved, you are inherently setting yourself up for turmoil. It can and will cause you to stumble in your Christian work and fall back into sin and water down the truth of God's Word. If you want to live right and be all that God has called you to be then, you need to choose the kind of company you keep. For the company you keep will ultimately determine the kind of life you will live. This is a choice you would have to make yourself!

Who are you yoked with?

Do not be unequally yoked with unbelievers [do not make mismated alliances with them or come under a different yoke with them, inconsistent with your faith]. For what partnership have right living and right standing with God with iniquity and lawlessness? Or how can light have fellowship with darkness? 2 Corinthians 6:14

Who are you yoked with? Or who are you becoming yoked with? Not too long and you will begin to think like them, dress like them, talk like them and eventually live like them. It has been said that bad influences have more effect on close relationships than good influences. We are called to refrain from close relationship with them. Friend, you are the light in the world, you are the salt of the earth, you were created for greatness, God has put so much inside of you. You are to be different from the world, now I said different not weird. You have a great destiny but only you can fulfil that destiny and it's a choice that only you can make!

Remember the story you just read, I would liken the scorpion to an unbeliever and the turtle a young Christian (this is just an analogy). Unbelievers have no control of what they do. They cannot change on their own; they cannot change the way they live and what they do. They are full of sin, which comes naturally for them because, that's who they are - sinners. No man can change themselves without God. Have you ever been in a situation where you knew you shouldn't be doing 'that thing' but you kept at it just because of your friends? Are you in a situation where you shouldn't be going 'into that place' but you went on just because of your friends?

If you choose to compromise your faith just to please your friends, how then would you have the boldness to pray for them and lead them to Christ? Can you see how easy it could be to walk away from your destiny instead of walking towards it? The law of association says that 'either you are becoming like them or they are becoming like you.' Who are you becoming like? Are your friends taking you to the clubs more than you are taking them to church, or are you going more to the club more than you are going to church, are you beginning to enjoy more of the world than the gospel, are you beginning to sound and speak more like them than they sound and speak like you, or are you beginning to talk with the world more than you talk with God? You need to evaluate yourself friend.

Blessed (happy, fortunate, prosperous and enviable) is the man who walks and lives not in the counsel of the ungodly [following their advice, their plans and purposes], nor stands [submissive and inactive] in the path where sinners walk, nor sits down [to relax and rest] where the scornful [and the mockers] gather. Psalms 1:1

Who then are you listening to? Are you taking counsel from people who don't even believe in the God you serve? Who despise the very essence of who you are? Have you not heard that birds of the same feather flock together? How can you stay comfortably with someone who is against everything you stand for?

2 Corinthians 6:17 says, to come out from among [unbelievers], and separate (sever) yourselves from them, says the Lord, and touch not [any] unclean thing.

To separate means "to set apart, to disunite, to divide, to part company, to go in a different direction, to cease to be associated with, to become distinct or disengaged, as cream separates from milk." To sever means to cut away from. This is all self explanatory. You must choose to rise above the world's system and standards, above the sinful lifestyle they live and do what the Word says in Romans 12:2 which says not to be conformed to this world and their way of thinking and doing things; but for you to be transformed to the way God desires for you to live which is according to His Word even by the renewing of your mind. In other words, don't live like them, talk like them and don't be them.

Friend it doesn't matter how long you have been together, you need to obey God rather than men. You see, sin has pleasure, we all know that. However, the pleasure is just for a season. Seasons come and seasons go but God's Word remains true forever. If you decide to remain in darkness and live your life contrary to God's Word, you will be living in sin. You must understand that if you continue to yield yourself to sin, you could become so entangled with it that you may lose your will power to repent and change. This not a route you want to follow. It is dangerous and would come with serious consequences. See Hebrew 6:4-9

You must know (recognize) that you were redeemed (ransomed) from the useless (fruitless) way of living inherited by tradition from [your] forefathers, not with corruptible things [such as] silver and gold, but [you were purchased] with the precious blood of Christ (the Messiah), like that of a [sacrificial] lamb without blemish or spot. 1 Peter 1:18-19

Who is influencing you?

The people you spend more of your time with will determine what kind of a person you will grow up to be. The right friends can be a blessing and empower you to succeed in life and the wrong ones can be a curse and empower you to fail. Good friends will motivate you to obey God and succeed in life. Who are you constantly hanging out with? Are they lovers of God? Are they honest people who tell you the truth? Or are they people who just tell you what you want to hear?

Proverbs 27:17 says, iron sharpens iron; so a man sharpens the countenance of his friend [to show rage or worthy purpose]. Who are your friends?

Are they influencing you to be a better person and be the best that you can be or are they drawing you away from the wonderful person that you truly are? Do your friends help you get closer to God or are they pulling you away from Him and gently taking you out of the will of God for your life? You must have standards for yourself friend. These standards must of course be based on God's Word. Now evaluate yourself, how careful are you about your choice of friends. How would you rate yourself as a friend? Do you measure up to the world's standards or God's standards?

The Word of God says concerning choosing friends that we should choose our friends carefully and stay away from foolish people. **Proverbs 13:20 says, He who walks [as a companion] with wise men is wise, but he who associates with [self-confident] fools is [a fool himself and] shall smart for it. Isaiah 32:6 says, for the fool speaks folly and his mind plans iniquity: practicing profane ungodliness and speaking error concerning the Lord, leaving the craving of the hungry unsatisfied and causing the drink of the thirsty to fail.**

To stay away from people who lose their temper easily. Proverbs 22:24 says, Make no friendship with a man given to anger, and with a wrathful man do not associate; and not to make friends with rebellious people. Proverbs 24:21 says ...do not associate with those who are given to change [of allegiance and revolutionary] or rebellious. Remember, sin and anointing do not and cannot dwell together!

Note the balance!

Now let me clarify this. The Word of God is not telling us not to interact with unbelievers, off course we are not supposed to isolate ourselves from them after all; we work with them, school with them, and do live amongst them. But the Bible tells us not to have close intimate relationships with them, to refrain from close relationship with them. We are in the world but are not of the world.

Let your light so shine before men that they may see your moral excellence and your praiseworthy, noble and good deeds and recognise and honour and praise and glorify your father who is in heaven. Matthew 5:16

And the servant of the Lord must not be quarrelsome (fighting and contending). Instead, he must be kindly to everyone and mild tempered [preserving the bond of peace]; he must be a skilled and suitable teacher, patient and forbearing and willing to suffer wrong. He must correct his opponents with courtesy and gentleness, in the hope that God may grant that they will repent and come to know the truth [that they will perceive and recognize and become accurately acquainted with and acknowledge it], and that they may

come to their senses [and] escape out of the snare of the devil, having been held captive by him, [henceforth] to do His [God's] will. **2 Timothy 2:24-26**

To open their eyes that they may turn from darkness to light and from the power of Satan to God, so that they may thus receive forgiveness and release from their sins and a place and portion among those who are consecrated and purified by faith in me. Acts 26:18

The Word of God says that we are to be kind to them and are to influence them and not to be influenced by them. Friend, God has given you the ministry of reconciliation. You are to reconcile the world back to God. You are called to be a light to them. Dare to shine! Your primary focus should be to share your faith with them and win them to Christ. Someone once said, "Well, I can have a very close relationship with an unbeliever and not get influenced by them. In fact, my best friend is an unbeliever and most of my very close friends are unbelievers. We go to night clubs together but I don't drink and smoke with them. I feel more comfortable with them than I even do with my Christian folks"

God cannot lie!

Dear friend, if this is the same view, you share then you do have a problem and really do need help. It is either you are the liar or you have just chosen not to believe God's Word. The devil is a liar, because God cannot lie! He said not to be unequally yoked with unbelievers remember! The Word of God remains true forever. If God's Word says not to be unequally yoked with unbelievers, you should not be unequally yoked with them. This shows a lack of reverence or fear for God. The Word of God says that the fear of the Lord is the beginning of knowledge. You see, the fear of God is what will bring you the promises of God; promises of God's protection, healing, and the blessings of God and so on which will cause you to shine in the midst of the darkness even this dark world we live in!

Don't you realize that this is not the way to live? Unjust people who don't care about God will not be joining in his kingdom. Those

who use and abuse each other, use and abuse sex, use and abuse the earth and everything in it, don't qualify as citizens in God's kingdom. A number of you know from experience what I'm talking about, for not so long ago you were on that list. Since then, you've been cleaned up and given a fresh start by Jesus, our Master, our Messiah, and by our God present in us, the Spirit. 1 Corinthians 6:9-10 (the message)

You cannot change anyone

You cannot change anyone, not even yourself. You didn't die for them either. Jesus died for them and He has put everything in place in His Word. Only God through the Holy Spirit can Change any man! Quit trying because you will never succeed. Just follow the Word of God. The Word of God shows that friendship is a covenant word. Please see James 2:23, Genesis 15:6, 2 Chronicles 20:7, Isaiah 41:8 making reference to Abraham as the friend of God. Someone once said that friendship is a relationship that gives you the advantage. If you have people in your life who are always and only concerned with what they can get from you, they are not true friends. You need to re evaluate that relationship.

Take a minute now and think about the friends you have, your relationships. Are they giving you the advantage? Are they influencing you positively or negatively? Are they bringing out the best in you and drawing you closer to God or do you find yourself compromising your faith whenever you are around them? Are there friends in your life right now that you have to break away from completely? You can decide the quality of life you would want to live and choose to surround yourself with the friends who represent and support that dream of yours and quality of life.

Choose to make friends with people who share the same values, principles and faith with you; People who will motivate you to fulfil your destiny. Who believe in you and your God given vision; friends who have a vision for themselves; friends who know that they are going somewhere, who have a dream and a vision and have a sharp focus on what they need to accomplish in life; friends who are sowers and who are passionate about God. Have friends who not only know the Word, but are doers of the Word.

Your destiny should be the most important thing to you. It's time to re evaluate your relationships and leave some friends behind and get new ones! God has called you into greatness, He has called you to solve a problem that only you can do well, and you are an answer to a problem God knew would arise in your time and generation. Do not allow anything or anyone stop you or hinder you from fulfilling that call upon your life. It's your call. Make the right choice today, right now. Be the difference; make a difference and Dare to shine!

Remember:

- Your friends have a heavy influence in your life whether you know it or not.
- Your friends should bring out the best in you and draw you closer to God; or do you find yourself compromising your faith whenever you are around them?
- You must have standards for yourself. These standards must of course be based on God's Word.
- You are called to be a light to them. Your primary focus should be to share the love of God and your faith with them and win them to Christ.
- Dare to make a difference, be the difference and DARE TO SHINE!

Think on these:

The people you spend more of your time with will determine what kind of a person you will grow up to be. The right friends can be a blessing and empower you to succeed in life and the wrong ones can be a curse and empower you to fail.

Your thoughts:

Study Questions

1. What does 1 Corinthians 15:33 say?

----

2. What influence do your friends have on you? Are these positive or negative influences?

----

3. Are your friendships in accordance with God's Word?

----

4. Are they leading you away from God or are you leading them to God?

----

5. Who are you accountable to? Your friends or God?

Principle #5
Dating and Sex – it's not for Kids!

The issue of Dating and sex is one that every Christian teenager, youth, single young man and woman should have a clear understanding of. It is so important. It's a decision you will make in life that could be a blessing or turn out to be a big problem for you. Remember, every decision or choice made has its consequences that would not only affect you, but could affect someone else. During the teen years of growth, we all as teenagers, go through a period of time in which we undergo some emotional and physical changes in our bodies, when we become aware of who we are (in terms of our sex) and what we have to offer the world. One of these changes is in the area of attraction to the opposite sex.

As a Christian teenager, youth, young man or woman, you need to learn first of all, to be proud of who you are and respect your body and your Faith; Have a good self image. You need to know that you are worthy of the love and affection of others, but you must never compromise your belief, values, your faith and love for God for anyone's love and affection. This is a choice you would have to make for yourself. Let's look into the issue of dating now.

What does the Word say about Dating?

The Word of God does not say anything about dating but it does describe and gives directions regarding relationships one of which is friendship. Dating is a method which people employ in the time and age we are in; to get to know others of the opposite sex that was not employed in Biblical times. Oh! Does it mean then that as Christians we are not allowed to date? That's not what I am saying. Yes, Christians can date. However, you must understand the purpose of dating and approach it from the perspective of the Word of God.

I will now give you two kinds of dating definitions. For some, the definition of dating is where two people of the opposite sex who are attracted to each other get together with the aim of building a relationship centred on romantic desires with physical intimacy. This is a definition based on the world's perception of dating. They see dating as 'something that is expected and a rite of passage, which brings them more maturity.'

The second definition of dating is where two people of the opposite sex who are attracted to each other get together with the aim of getting to know each other in order to build a solid relationship without the involvement of romantic desires with physical intimacy. This should be the Christian perception of dating. As you can see it is quite different from the world's perception of dating. Christians see it as more of an honour and a way to build a life with someone once they are mature. Dear friend, Christian dating is also based on building a productive relationship with God as well. Therefore instead of just answering to yourself, your parents, someone else or the person you are dating, you are also answering to God.

The whole purpose of Christian dating should be to enjoy each other's company as you build meaningful, healthy relationship that enables you to share love with each other; the kind of love described in the Bible, a love that is based on God's standards and then apply this in your relationship.

1 Corinthians 13:4-7 says: Love endures long and is patient and kind; love never is envious nor boils over with jealousy, is not boastful or vainglorious, does not display itself haughty. It is not conceited (arrogant and inflated with pride); it is not rude (unmannerly) and does not act unbecomingly. Love (God's love in us) does not insist on its own rights or its own way, for it is not self-seeking; it is not touchy or fretful or resentful; it takes no account of the evil done to it [it pays no attention to a suffered wrong]. It does not rejoice at injustice and unrighteousness, but rejoices when right and truth prevail. Love bears up under anything and everything that comes, is ever ready to believe the best of every person, it's hopes are fadeless under all circumstances, and it endures everything [with out weakening]. Love never fails.

Any relationship that is not based on the Word of God is not a healthy relationship which you need to break and come out of. The Bible is the manual for our spiritual growth. Dear friend, you've got to understand that finding the right person is not just about finding a great date to the prom; it is not just about finding that slim tall beautiful girl, or tall handsome guy, it is not just about their good looks, it is finding the person who shares your values, principles and faith with you and respects them; and who is ready and willing to conform to them no matter the cost.

How then should Christians date?

It is important that you are mature enough to follow God's Word and standards for relationship and be ready for it.

Making a choice to date only a believer is a very important step you should take. One who loves the Lord and has a real relationship with Him. Never ever date an unbeliever with the intention to convert him/her or your date may not be willing to conform to your Christian beliefs which would not end up well in your favour. This is against the Word of God and will weaken your relationship with God and compromise your morals and standards.

Do not be yoked together with unbelievers. For what do righteousness and wickedness have in common? Or what fellowship can light have with darkness? What harmony is there between Christ and Belial? What does a believer have in common with an unbeliever? 2 Corinthians 6:14-15 (NKJ) See also Philippians 2:5.

Make the choice to put God first above any other relationship. "**He who loves [and takes more pleasure in] father or mother more than [in] me is not worthy of me; and he who loves [and takes more pleasure in] son or daughter more than [in] me is not worthy of Me." Matthew 10:37** To say or believe that another person is everything or the most important thing in one's life above God is idolatry and that's a sin. Please read Galatians 5:20, Colossians 3:5.

Words of wisdom for dating

Never date anyone who wants you to change for them or makes you compromise your faith in God. Know the kind of person you would love to spend your life with. Know their character. Don't just assume that because he or she said that he/she is a believer that they truly are. The Bible says that, by their fruits you shall know them. Not by what they say or claim. Be open to other possibilities. In other words, don't settle for the first person that comes your way, take your time before agreeing to a date. Remain honest at all times, no matter what. Be sure that they are honest too.

Honesty is the basis of any good lasting relationship and it should be the basis of all your friendship and or dating. Do bear in mind too that as you have your conversations about certain issues, you don't always have to agree on everything as long as it's not an important issue. However, you do need to be able to talk about it, even if you have differing opinions.

Discuss issues like sex and marriage early before it becomes an issue. This is necessary for compatibility reasons as well. Do they believe in the sanctity of marriage? Do they understand that marriage is a covenant that God intends to last a lifetime no matter what? What do they believe about the issue of divorce? Do they think that you should have sex before marriage? It's very important that you discuss these issues at the early stages of your relationship.

If you don't share the same views about it, be careful.

Make the choice to set your priorities right. You must know your limitations. Set boundaries for yourself especially about sex, alcohol, drugs, fondling, and heavy petting; romantic intimacy with physical contact. Set boundaries on where you go together, what movies you watch together and the people you hang around with. Be accountable to somebody you look up to. Make this all of these very clear to your date from the very beginning of the relationship. A young man once said,

"I made up my mind from the beginning of my relationship with my date never to spend the night with her. As we usually did late night studies together, we both agreed that no matter what, we would not go to each other's rooms when it was late. We kept to these for a couple of weeks until one night, after our study, she asked if I would like a cup of tea and biscuits at her place. I hesitated knowing that I had set that boundary but she kept on insisting that it was just a cup of tea and nothing else. I knew I shouldn't, but I just wanted to please her, so I agreed and went into her room that night, but said I wouldn't waste anytime there. We got talking and one gist led to another. To cut the long story short, we ended up having sex together. I feel so bad about it and can't even look her in the eye. I don't think I really want to continue with that relationship anymore, as I always feel a sense of guilt whenever I am with her"

You see, setting boundaries and understanding the purpose of these boundaries would help you and protect you from falling into temptation in your relationship. However, you must make a decision to commit to these boundaries. It's not just enough to say something or set boundaries, you MUST COMMIT to it no matter the cost! Most people make new year resolutions, but how many of you know that, it's not the making that matters, it's the commitment to it, the doing it that would produce the result!

Make a choice to listen to your godly parents. The Bible says for you to obey your parents in the Lord. God has given them wisdom to help you and to guide you. I know a lot of you think that you know it all, but that's not true. Listen to them. They have been there before and can see beyond what you can see in your date. Listen to the Holy Spirit in you when He speaks to you regarding your decisions even in this area of dating. Remember, He knows all things. Obey Him. And have fun but remember your fun should be within the boundaries of God's Word.

Let's talk about Sex and Sexual intimacy

Let's talk about Sex! Yes you heard that right. We live in a generation where sex is seen in every medium. It's now in every movie, magazine, TV show, talk show, news paper and internet. It is the point of a lot of music and condoms are now being handed out in schools. (Lord have mercy) Society today makes it seem as though pre marital sex (sex outside of a marriage relationship) is okay because it feels good. This is completely wrong. Sex is not for kids! Get married first! However, sex is a good thing.

Sex is indeed a good thing. Are you serious? Yes! However, God created sex for a husband and wife to express their love for one another.

Genesis 2:23-25; Proverbs 5:18-19 says, let your fountain [of human life] be blessed [with the rewards of fidelity], and rejoice in the wife of your youth. Let her be as the loving hind and pleasant doe [tender, gentle, attractive], let her bosom satisfy you at all times, and always be transported with delight in her love.

God wants you to hold your passion and wait until you are married. 1 Corinthians 7:2-3. **But because of the temptation to impurity and to avoid immorality, let each [man] have his own wife and let each [woman] have her own husband.** It is therefore very important that as Christian teens and youth, that you know what the Bible says about it and have a clear understanding. This can help you live without guilt and keep you pure and focused.

What then is sexual intimacy?

It's been said and very true too that, Sexual intimacy is more than just the act of sexual intercourse. (Penetration) It is by its very nature any physical contact which stimulates a sexual response in either partner even if nakedness is not uncovered. Sexual intimacy is not just an act; it is a whole process of developing physical intimacy. Engaging in activity of this nature with someone outside of marriage is sexual immorality. Friend, this kind of relationship should be avoided by all means and at all costs.

Shun immorality and all sexual looseness [flee from impurity in thought, word or deed]. Any other sin which a man commits is one outside the body, but he who commits sexual immorality sins against his own body. Do you not know that your body is the temple (the very sanctuary) of the Holy Spirit who lives within you, whom you have received [as a Gift] from God? You are not your own, you were bought with a price [purchased with a preciousness and paid for, made His own]. So then, honour God and bring glory to Him in your body. 1 Corinthians 6:18-20

Dear friend, sexual immorality is a sin not only against God but also against your own body. You should love and honour others as you love yourself. Let me stress this again. The purpose of God in giving man and woman the ability to experience romantic and physical intimacy with each other was for marriage. It was not for a relationship outside of marriage.

Let marriage be held in honour (esteemed worthy, precious, of great price, and especially dear) in all things. And thus let the marriage bed be undefiled (kept undis-honoured); for God will judge and punish the unchaste [all guilty of sexual vice] and adulterous. Child of God, sexual intimacy is a meaningful and beautiful thing but is meant to be experienced by married couples only.

Ephesians 5:31 says, for this cause shall a man leave his father and mother and shall b e joined unto his wife, and they two shall be one flesh.

Sadly a lot of teenagers, youth, young men and women are already having sexual intercourse or sexual intimacy without realising the emotional, physical and spiritual consequences. There are consequences. Sexual relations will never meet the deep emotional needs of either partner, but the emotional scarring and damage of casual sex can take a lifetime to heal if you are not careful.

Proverbs 6:27-28 says can a man take fire in his bosom and his clothes not be burned? Can one go upon hot coals and his feet not be burned? Proverbs 9:17-18 says, stolen waters (pleasures) are sweet [because they are forbidden]; and bread eaten in secret is pleasant.

Proverbs 20:17 says, food gained by deceit is sweet to a man, but afterward his mouth will be filled with gravel.

Dear friend, as a Christian teenager or youth, I know you do fight temptation every day. We all do even as adults. Being tempted is not the sin, but giving into the temptation is. It is only by relying on God for strength that you can truly fight off the temptation.

For no temptation (no trial regarded as enticing to sin), [no matter how it comes or where it leads] has overtaken you and laid hold on you that is not common to man [that is, no temptation or trial has come to you that is beyond human resistance and that is not adjusted and adapted and belonging to human experience, and such as man can bear]. But God is faithful [to His Word and to His compassionate nature], and He [can be trusted] not to let you be tempted and tried and assayed beyond your ability and strength of resistance and power to endure, but with the temptation He will [always] also provide the way out (the means of escape to a landing place), that you may be capable and strong and powerful to bear up under it patiently. 1 Corinthians 10:13

Peer Pressure? No Way!

Dear friend, please do not give into peer pressure when they say that 'everyone is doing it'. This is not true. You are not everyone, neither is your name called everyone. And for your information, not everyone is doing it. Are you sure? Yes! However, so what if everyone is doing it. You are a covenant child of God. You are different, you were bought with the precious blood of Jesus; your body is the temple of the Holy Spirit. Learn to stand for what is right and be an example to your peers. God has called you to be a light unto them. They are to look up to you and follow you, not the other way round. Avoid any relationship that tends to lead you into falling into this temptation. The Word of God says to flee all appearances of evil. Avoid heavy petting and fondling. This is a dangerous act as it can lead you into the actual act of sex. Are you serious? Yes I am. Why set yourself up to be tempted? Why set yourself up for trouble? '

Friend, if you are in a date and your date wants you to have sex with him/her, please refuse this request! A young girl once said that her date asked her if they could have sex together. She said no, that, it was not right to do that as they were not married. This carried on for a while until one day; he said to her that, if she really loved him, then she should prove it to him by agreeing to have sex with him. She got so confused, she came and told me about it saying that, if she didn't agree, she would lose him and she wasn't ready to lose him as she loved him. I call this emotional blackmail. Sadly, this is still going on

58

amongst teenagers, youth, young men and women. Sometimes it's the girl making the threat to leave and sometimes it's the guy.

Hear me now and please hear me well. If any guy or girl should ask you to have sex with them, Christian or unbeliever, please say a massive NO, THANK YOU! And walk away. You need to keep off from that person. It is a dangerous path to tread on. Your decision to go to bed or not to go to bed with that person is of great importance to your future and your destiny. It is greater than you can ever realise. If you make the wrong choice, you may regret it for the rest of your life if you are not careful. If you have sex before marriage, it is a sin unto God. And a sin to your own body as previously mentioned. It is God's will and purpose that you abstain from all manner of sexual immorality.

For this is the will of God, that you should be consecrated (separated and set apart for pure and holy living); that you should abstain and shrink from all sexual vice, that each one of you should know how to possess (control, manage) his own body in consecration (purity, separated from things profane) and honour. 1 Thessalonians 4:3-5

But immorality (sexual vice) and all impurity [of lustful, rich, wasteful living] or greediness must not even be named among you, as is fitting and proper among saints (God's consecrated people). Ephesians 5:3

Dangerous ground – Keep off!

If anybody uses sex as a tool to manipulate you as a way of proving your love for them, that person does not truly love you. They are just selfish, greedy and wicked and will eventually dump you like a used filthy rag! If they loved you, they would not be asking you to go against God's Word and against His will for both of you. He/she is not thinking about you at all but about their emotional needs and selfish desires. 1 Corinthians 13:5 says that love is not self seeking. Neither are they concerned about God and about pleasing Him. God doesn't really matter to them. They are a compromising people without integrity. Flee from such ones or they would ruin your life and destiny. Remember what we talked about in choosing your friends?

It is not conceited (arrogant and inflated with pride); it is not rude (unmannerly) and does not act unbecomingly. Love (God's love in us) does not insist on its own rights or its own way, for it is not self seeking; it is not touchy or fretful or resentful; it takes no account of the evil done to it [it pays no attention to a suffered wrong]. 1 Corinthians 13:5

It's an evil thing to want to make you sin against God. The Word of God says that love does not delight in evil. He/she doesn't care about God and if that's the case, you can be sure that he/she can't be bothered about caring about you. Ultimately, he/she cannot love you the way God wants you to be loved. Child of God, are you more concerned about what your friends says above what God says? Are you more concerned about pleasing your date, boyfriend/girlfriend or fiancée to pleasing God? Do you not know that when you choose to please your friend rather than pleasing God, when you choose to obey your friend rather than obeying God, you make that person your God? Don't tread on dangerous ground! Please Don't.

Why do you call me, Lord, Lord, and do not [practice] what I tell you? For everyone who comes to me and listens to my Words [in order to heed their teaching] and does them, I will show you what he is like: he is like a man building a house, who dug and went down deep and laid a foundation upon the rock; and when a flood arose, the torrent broke against that house and could not shake or move it, because it had been securely built or founded on a rock. But he who merely hears and does not practice doing my Words, is like a man who built a house on the ground without a foundation, against which the torrent burst, and immediately it collapsed and fell, and the breaking and ruin of that house was great. Luke 6:46

On what foundation are you building?

On what foundation are you building your life and relationship? Don't put your date, boyfriend or girlfriend above God! You are not to put anything and anyone above God. Remember, the Word of God says don't be misled: No one makes a fool of God. What a person plants, he will harvest. The person who plants selfishness, ignoring God; Harvests a crop of weeds. All he'll have to show for his life is weeds! Galatians 6:7 (The message) do not break your fellowship with Almighty God because of anybody and end up living a life of guilt and shame which will cause you to have a low self esteem. What if you get pregnant? What if you contract a terrible infection, STD (Sexually transmitted diseases) or even AIDS? It's not worth the stress my dear; it's not worth it at all! Come on, you are better than that. Walk away, the grace of God is sufficient for you.

For no temptation (no trial regarded as enticing to sin), [no matter how it comes or where it leads] has overtaken you and laid hold on you that is not common to man [that is, no temptation or trial has come to you that is beyond human resistance and that is not adjusted and adapted and belonging to human experience, and such as man can bear]. But God is faithful [to His Word and to His compassionate nature], and He [can be trusted] not to let you be tempted and tried and assayed beyond your ability and strength of resistance and power to endure, but with the temptation He will [always] also provide the way out (the means of escape to a landing place), that you may be capable and strong and powerful to bear up under it patiently. 1 Corinthians 10:13

Friend, do not allow anyone put pressure on you to do the wrong thing. Walk away from peer pressure; rather put pressure on your pressure with the Word of God! If they can't wait until you both are married, they are not the right persons for you. Break that relationship, call it off. It's just not worth it at all. The moment you start compromising your standards and values and go contrary to God's will for you just to please somebody, you may end up in a vicious circle that may be difficult to break and stop. The word 'NO' is so powerful. Use it! God loves you so much and cares about you. He wants you to have the best in life, so you can be a light in the darkness that shines so bright. God believes in you!

Isn't sex and love the same? You may ask; Most certainly not my dear. They are two completely different things. Sex is more of an act, love is an emotion and I must tell you, it's pretty dangerous and complex to mix up these two. You must never ever believe that to show love to your date or friend, that you have to have sex. It's a lie from the pit of hell. There are better and safer ways to show love to your friend without any romantic physical contact. What if we just have oral sex? Are you serious! What's up with you? Friend, let me burst your bubble. Oral sex is sex. Yes it is, period! You see, having sex is not just about the act, it is also about the frame of mind. However, oral sex is still a sexual act anyway. It is an act that bonds a man and woman together.

"What about watching porn or looking at pornographic magazines? That's not having sex is it?" You may ask. Dear friend, don't even go that way, don't dabble into that area. It is a dreadful part to walk on. As a teenager, youth, young man or woman, I need to let you know that you are treading on dangerous ground watching or reading pornography. Don't cross that line. It's not worth it. Pornography can become an addiction even worse than drugs.

Studies have proven that, it is a behavioural addiction as strong as cocaine. It will ruin your life now and in the future if you are not careful. Like I mentioned earlier, having sex is not just about the act, it's also about the frame of your mind. As you watch or look at that pornography, you are already committing sin because you are already lusting in your heart. Draw that line never to go this way and commit to it. I would even ask you to be very selective of what you and your date watch in terms of movies. That's why Jesus said in Matthew 5:28,

But I say to you that everyone who so much as looks at a woman with evil desire for her has already committed adultery with her in his heart.

You know the next commandment pretty well, too: 'Don't go to bed with another's spouse'. But don't think you've preserved your virtue simply by staying out of bed. Your heart can be corrupted by lust even quicker than your body. Those leering looks you think nobody notices – they also corrupt. (The message)

It's never too late to change!

What if I have already had sex outside of marriage? Will God ever forgive me? Is it too late to change? No, no, no, it's never too late!

It's never too late to repent and start a new leave in your life and relationship with God. God still loves you so very much. He hates the sin but He loves you as He loves Jesus. Nothing will and can change His love for you. Remember David in the Bible and how he committed adultery and the rest? When David realised his mistake, he genuinely repented before God and chose to start a new leave in his relationship with God. The Bible records that God called him (David) a man after His own heart. You can make the choice to make a fresh start right now. God is willing and eager to forgive you.

If we [freely] admit that we have sinned and confess our sins, He is faithful and just (true to His own nature and promises) and will forgive our sins [dismiss our lawlessness] and [continuously] cleanse us from all unrighteousness [everything not in conformity to His will in purpose, thought and action]. 1 John 1:9

You can obtain God's forgiveness, but you would have to ask for it and receive it. Wherever you are right now, you can ask God to forgive you. He's just a prayer away. Dear friend, regardless of what is going on in our society, stay focussed on the Word. Abstain from sexual immorality. Do not allow yourself to be put under pressure. Walk away, run away if you have to. The Bible says to flee from every appearance of evil. Sex before marriage is an evil thing before God! Keep and guard your heart with all diligence. Be the difference and make a difference. Dare to shine!

Proverbs 4:25 says let your eyes look right on [with fixed purpose], and let your gaze be straight before you. Consider well the path of your feet, and let all your ways be established and ordered aright. Turn not to the right hand or to the left: remove thy foot from evil.

Remember:

- You need to know that you are worthy of the love and affection of others, but you must never compromise your belief, values, your faith and love for God for anyone's love and affection.

- Never ever date an unbeliever with the intention to convert him/her or your date may not be willing to conform to your Christian beliefs which would not end up well in your favour.

- If you are in a date and your date wants you to have sex with him/her, please refuse!

- There are better and safer ways to show love to your friend without any romantic physical contact.

Think on these:

What is love according to 1 Corinthians 13?

- **Love is patient**
- **Love is kind**
- **Love is not envious**
- **Love does not boast**
- **Love is humble**
- **Love is not rude**
- **Love is not self seeking**
- **Love is not easily angered**
- **Love keeps no record of wrong**
- **Love is truthful**
- **Love protects**
- **Love trusts**
- **Love never fails!**

Your thoughts:

Study Questions

1. What is Christian Dating?

---

2. What is an unhealthy relationship according to God's Word?

---

3. What is sexual immorality according to the Word of God?

---

4. Summarise what 2 Corinthians 6:14-15 says

---

5. Evaluating your relationship, is it in line with God's standards?

Principle #6
Vision – Define your destination!

I was speaking to a young girl at the University a while ago, and I said to her, so tell me, what's your dream? What's your vision for your life? And what do you want to accomplish? When you look at your future, what do you see? She looked at me rather strangely, looked at the ground, looked up as though staring at something in the sky for a couple of minutes, looked up at me again and then said, "I really don't know yet. It's not really something I think about" Having spoken to quite a number of young people about this area, it is so amazing to know that a lot of teenagers, youth, young men and women do not yet have a vision for their lives. In fact, they do not even understand what a vision is all about and why they should have one.

Dear friend, imagine planning a trip to drive across the country without a destination in mind. What do you think would happen...? Quite right! You would just end up driving around aimlessly. Vision is everything. Without a vision of who you are, who you want to be and what you want to achieve in life, you will get stagnant, with no drive and sense of accomplishment. In other words, your vision is what will inspire you to achieve or accomplish anything. It helps you to know who you want to be, what you want to do and why you do the things you do. It's so sad to know that a lot of young men, women, youth and teenagers, are living their lives without purpose; as on a never ending treadmill and are barely able to keep up with the pace.

Proverbs 29:18 says, where there is no vision [no redemptive revelation of God], the people perish; but he who keeps the law [of God, which includes that of man] blessed (happy, fortunate and enviable) is he.

What is vision?

The NIV translation says, where there is no revelation, the people cast off restraint. The Message says if people can't see what God is doing, they stumble all over themselves. A vision can be said to be a reality that has yet to come into existence; it is like a force within, compelling a person or people to action. The word vision means to have sight, to dream, to imagine, and to receive revelation, it means enlightenment. By sight, I am not talking about our physical eyes, but the sight of the heart, the sight of the spirit. Remember, we live by faith and not by sight. Hebrews 10:38.

Someone defined vision as the capacity to see further than your eyes can look; the capacity to see beyond the barriers. The ability to see tomorrow before it comes. That it is the art of seeing what is invisible to others. That, your eyes show you what is, but vision shows you what can be. In other words, God wants us to live according to the vision of our hearts and not by our physical eyes.

"The most pathetic person in the world is someone who has sight, but has no vision!" – Helen Keller

To be without a vision, is to be like a sheep without a shepherd. To be without a vision is like having a touch light with no power, no battery in it. Someone once said, show me someone who doesn't know where he wants to go, and I will show you someone who won't go very far. Having a vision would make you prepared, instead of just being taken by surprise. A vision is an image that you have in your mind of your expected future. Do you have a vision for your life?

Dear friend, you may have all the talents in the world and have great gifts in you but if you do not have a vision for your life, it would all be a waste. Great men and women on this earth know what they want and achieved such great success because they had a dream, a vision and dared to pursue it. Success has nothing to do with chance or luck. Success is something you create for yourself. You can only do this by having a vision. All successful people have a vision. A vision can take you from the lows to great heights, from obscurity to stardom, from poverty to prosperity, from failure to success, from hell to heaven.

Vision opens the door to the maximisation of life! It's been said that life is a journey, which must be defined by a vision. God does not despise small beginnings, but without a vision, you cannot have true success. Child of God, what choices are you making about your future? What vision do you have regarding your career, your education, ministry, relationship, health, job, business and the list goes on and on. Suffice to say that, it's not just enough for you to have a vision for the future. Be sure that your vision is in line with God's will for your life.

Proverbs 19:21 says, many plans are in a man's mind, but it is the Lord's purpose for him that will stand. Is the vision you have in line with God's plan for you? Galatians 5:7 says, you were running superbly, who cut in on you, deflecting you from the true course of obedience? (The message)

Do you know God's plan and purpose for your life? If yes, what then are you doing about it? And if no, when would you begin to do something about knowing it? You see, if you are disobedient to what God has spoken over your life, you will not progress beyond your last act of obedience.

Jeremiah 29:11 says, for I know the thoughts and plans that I have for you, says the Lord, thoughts and plans for welfare and peace and not evil, to give you hope in your final outcome. It is a tragedy to live life without a purpose. To wake up every morning and not know why God created you. God has plans to give you the future you hope for. Jeremiah 1:5 says, before I formed you in the womb I knew [and] approved of you [as my chosen instrument], and before you were born I separated and set you apart...

You have a great destiny

Child of God, God has an awesome plan and purpose for your life. You were created with a purpose and a destiny, to be a joy and fulfilment to somebody. You were born to fulfil an assignment, to deliver something to your generation and to be a solution to someone else's problem. That's why He placed that gifting in you. The anointing of God upon your life is not for you, it's for someone else out there. Don't waste it, use it!

However, you have to understand that our enemy, the devil does not want you to know about your purpose let alone fulfil it, and so he will do everything possible to try and distract you or completely stop you from fulfilling your destiny. But the devil is a liar! This is why you must have a vision, be a person of vision. Having a vision, will help you run the race with a purpose, with a target in mind and not just running without any form of direction. Vision gives you a dream to pursue and a gaol to achieve. Vision is what will help you to overcome seemingly insurmountable obstacles and keep you holding on when times are hard and the going gets tough.

1 Corinthians 16:13 says, keep your eyes open, hold tight to your convictions, give it all you've got, be resolute and love without stopping. (The message Bible)

Someone once said that, if you have vision, you have purpose. If you have purpose, you have direction. Knowing all of these, you would not waste your time on activities and things that will not get you to your destination. There is no room for procrastination. Procrastination is a thief and a killer of dreams! If you can only understand the vision that God has given you as a Christian, then and only then would you realise your uniqueness, your footprint and only then can you move and become all that God has called you and wants you to be.

Proverbs 19:21 says, many plans are in a man's mind, but it is the Lord's purpose for him that will stand.

You will never be happy or satisfied until you do what God has called you to do and accomplish. This is a hard saying, but it's the truth. It's like running a race and getting to the finish line, only to be disqualified because you were running on the wrong lane. Therefore, make your plans according to God's purpose if not, you may end up wasting precious time and energy in the wrong direction. Somebody once said that, if you do not know your vision, you would end up pursuing other people's visions. That is a tragedy.

Write your vision down.

Habakkuk 2:2 says, write the vision and engrave it so plainly upon tablets that everyone who passes may [be able to] read [it easily and quickly] as he hastens by. The message says, write what you see.

When you look at your future what do you see? Have you defined your vision, have you written it down? One of the ways to be successful in your vision is to visualize it, write it down, and set goals and a plan of action to reach it. When you are able to do this, your vision will consume you with a sense of responsibility. A lot of people say that they have a vision, but it's in their head. For some reason, they don't just write it down. If the Word of God says for you to write your vision down, then write it down. Obey the Word!

Do you know that when you do not write your vision down it is just a wish? Writing your vision down will also make you accountable to yourself and others. It has been said that, the difference between a leader and a daydreamer is that the leader activates his dreams, while the daydreamer just thinks about them. Child of God, God has put the seed of leadership and greatness in you but you need to develop it.

Someone once said that, the reason so many individuals fail to achieve their goals in life is that they never really set them in the first place. Writing your vision down will make it clearer and give you more understanding of it as you look at it daily. Speak about your dream. Now am not saying that you should tell every dick, tom or harry about it, speak it to yourself! There is power in your tongue, for your words have creative power in them. Speak your dreams to God. Remind Him of His promises to you concerning dream. If God gave you that dream, He will cause it to come to pass. You may speak to others about it but be sure who you share it with. Some people are dream killers!

You shall also decide and decree a thing, and it shall be established for you; and the light [of God's favour] shall shine upon your ways. Job 22:28

Set goals for your vision

It is so very important for you to set goals for your vision because, goals will instil a drive in you to fulfil your purpose or vision. Your goals decide what is important to you. It will help keep you organised, focused and keep you from been distracted, or side tracked by anyone or anything. It will constantly remind you why you chose to do what you are doing, why you are doing it and how you would accomplish it

Hebrews 12:2 says looking away [from all that will distract] to Jesus, who is the leader and the source of our faith [giving the first incentive for our belief] and is also it's finisher [bringing it to maturity and perfection]. He, for the joy [of obtaining the prize] that was set before Him, endured the cross, despising and ignoring the shame, and is now seated at the right hand of the throne of God.

Jesus had a clearly defined goal and kept His total focus on it to the end. **Look 19:10 says 'For the Son of man came to seek and to save that which was lost'.** Make the choice today to set goals for your life. And commit to it.

"In whatever position you find yourself, determine your objective first. Until your thoughts are linked to a purpose there can be no accomplishment. There is no achievement without goals. If you don't know where you are going, how can you expect to get there? The world has the habit of making room for the person whose words and actions show that they know where they are going. Goals give you a starting place and a destination. With them, you will be able to determine what it will cost you to get there. In your pursuit of them, you will be going somewhere. Only you can determine what you want. You can decide on your major objectives, targets and aims. Knowing where you are going is all you need to get there." –author unknown

Proverbs 21:5 says careful planning puts you ahead in the long run; hurry and scurry puts you further behind. (The message)

The Bible is not against setting goals. You can and should set goals for your life as a Christian. Set your goals according to the will of God for your life.

How to set your Goals

Take out a sheet of paper or a note book and ask yourself what you would like to accomplish in life. In other words, if you had no limits in life, what would you like to achieve? Do some good brainstorming and then begin to put all of the things, ideas and thoughts in your mind on the sheet of paper or note book. Now follow this few steps:

- Write them down. This would help you to remain focused and not get distracted.

- Your goals should be challenging and demanding, goals that will really stretch you. However, they must be realistic and achievable. If it is not challenging then you're not really doing anything out of the ordinary. Make goals that will push you and require you to put in your best effort.

- Your goals must be clear. Do not write vague goals. Anyone should be able to look at it and understand where you are going and what you want to achieve.

- Prioritise your goals. Know which must be done first

- Set yourself a deadline and a time to accomplish them or it. However, this should be realistic.

- Evaluate your progress. Have a sense of measuring your progress, so you would know when it has been achieved.

- Remain motivated. Do not give up or quit.

Knowing the Vision of God for your life

But if from there you will seek (inquire for and require as necessity) the Lord your God, you will find Him if you [truly] seek Him with all your heart [and mind] and soul and life. Deuteronomy 4:29

How do I know the Vision of God for my life you may ask? There may be some other ways, but one of the most powerful ways to know the vision of God for your life is to spend quality time with God consistently, reading the Word of God and spending time in prayer and consecration. Listening to the voice of the Holy Spirit in you, only He can reveal it to you. Sometimes, God would reveal it to you by placing a desire in your heart concerning it and God may also speak through somebody to tell you by way of prophesy. You may also get a witness in your heart that agrees with what you were told. However, you must have the desire to want to know the Vision of God for your life.

Psalm 37:5 says, commit your way to the Lord [roll and repose each care of your load on Him]; trust (lean on, rely on, and be confident) also in Him and He will bring it to pass.

Never ever give up

Everyone has a dream but sadly, only a few achieve their dreams. This is because; some just decided to give up, to quit. Some are not so sure any more and begin to wonder if it was actually from God and if it was ever possible to achieve it. Some quit because of other people's opinions about them or about that dream; and some quit because of challenges they face. Friend, Joseph had a dream. He was so excited about it, was filled with passion and full of joy about his dream.

You all know the story of Joseph and his dreams and how he ended up as a slave boy and later into prison. But guess what, Joseph didn't give up on his dream regardless of people's opinions about him, regardless of the challenges he faced. Joseph saw his dream come to pass! How awesome. Why have you given up on your dreams? Please realise that nobody can stop you from achieving that dream, that vision of yours. You are the only one who can. Not even the devil can stop it. He may try and circumstances may try but these will not succeed.

"For you have need of steadfast patience and endurance, so that you may perform and fully accomplish the will of God, and thus

receive and carry away [and enjoy to the full] what is promised. But our way is not that of those who draw back to eternal misery (perdition) and are utterly destroyed, but we are of those who believe [who cleave to and trust in and rely on God through Jesus Christ, the Messiah] and by faith preserve the soul" Hebrew 10:36, 39

Friend, do not quit. If God gave you that dream, that vision, He is able to bring it to pass in your life. Pick up yourself right now. Begin to dream again. Step out in faith and walk into your destiny. You see, Joseph's dream looked as though it would never come to pass. But Joseph never gave up, he never quit and he never stopped trusting God. I believe he kept on speaking to himself about his dream and reminding God about his dream. It came to pass! Believe in yourself, believe God and trust Him to see it come to pass.

Put your confidence in God

Make the decision today to put your trust in God and not in any man to see your vision and goals accomplished.

Jeremiah 17:7-8 says [most] blessed is the man who believes in, trusts in, and relies on the Lord, and whose hope and confidence the Lord is. For he shall be like a tree planted by the waters that spreads out its roots by the river; and it shall not see and fear when heat comes; but its leaf shall be green. It shall not be anxious and full of care in the year of drought, nor shall it cease yielding fruit.

You must trust God and not your ability for it is not by your power or by your might that you can accomplish anything good in life. It is by the Spirit of God through His grace. Trust God to bring your vision and goals into manifestation. Put all your trust in Him, wait on Him and do your part of preparation as you wait for the manifestation to come.

Habakkuk 2:3 says, for the vision is yet for an appointed time and it hastens to the end [fulfilment]; it will not deceive or disappoint. Though it tarry, wait [earnestly] for it, because it will surely come; it will not be behindhand on its appointed day.

"In whatever position you find yourself determine your objective first. Until your thoughts are linked to a purpose there can be no accomplishment. There is no achievement without goals. If you don't know where you are going, how can you expect to get there? The world has the habits of making room for the person whose words and actions show that they know where they are going. Goals give you a starting place and a destination. With them, you will be able to determine what it will cost you to get there. In your pursuit of them, you will be going someplace. Only you can decide on your major objectives, targets, and aims. Knowing where you are going is all you need to get there." - Author Unknown.

Remember, no matter your present circumstances, you can be a success in life. For your present circumstances or situations do not determine where you can go or what you can accomplish in life, but they merely determine your starting point or place. The Word of God says that, God has given everyone of us the measure of grace. Begin today to walk in that grace and grow in it. It has been said that, whatever is conceivable is attainable! Vision is the key to your life having meaning. Make the choice today to live a life of vision and do something great with your life. Be the difference; make a difference and Dare to shine!

Remember:

- Having a vision, will help you run the race with a purpose, with a target in mind and not just running without any form of direction. Vision gives you a dream to pursue and a gaol to achieve.

- It helps you to know who you want to be, what you want to do and why you do the things you do.

- You may have all the talents in the world and have great gifts in you but if you do not have a vision for your life, it would all be a waste.

- It has been said that, the difference between a leader and a daydreamer is that the leader activates his dreams, while the daydreamer just thinks about them.

Think on these:

The worst failure on earth is not failure to marry, failure to buy your dream house, your dream car, or win the lottery. The worst failure is not failure to go to the University, study the course of your dreams or come out with a first class degree. The worst failure on earth is failure to fulfil the destiny God has called you to accomplish. To live life without a vision!

Your thoughts:

Study Questions

1. What do you see and where are you going in life?

----

2. What do you understand by vision?

----

3. What is the plan or purpose of God for your life?

----

4. Do you have a vision for your life? Have you written it down?

----

5. What are your goals in accomplishing your vision? Make a
   list of them below.

Principle #7

Purpose – Get a grip on your purpose!

Have you ever asked yourself the question why God created you and why you are alive today? You see, until you know the answers to this question, you may never find real fulfilment in life no matter what you do.

"Before I shaped you in the womb, I knew all about you. Before you saw the light of day, I had holy plans for you: A prophet to the nations that's what I had in mind for you." Jeremiah 1:5 (the message)

You weren't born into the world by mistake. No, you were not a mistake. God had a plan and a purpose for your life. You were placed on the earth for a PURPOSE! A number of people, teenagers and youth have recognised their purpose on earth and are walking in it, while quite a number haven't. Sadly, some have quit and have given up, while some are still trying to find their purpose.

What is purpose?

Purpose has been defined as the reason for which something exists, is done, made or used. Someone defined it as the original intent for the creation of a thing that was in the mind of the creator of the thing. That it is the 'why' for a thing. And it has been said that, where purpose is not known, abuse is inevitable. Friend, true success is knowing your purpose, knowing that thing that God has called you to do and fulfilling it. The Bible says that,

Many plans are in a man's mind, but it is the Lord's purpose for him that will stand. Proverbs 19:21

Do you know your purpose in God? It has been said that the wealthiest place on earth is the cemetery. Why? Because, people die and are buried with their purpose, gifting, talents, and all the great ideas, inventions and creativity that man could ever know; all never achieved or fulfilled. You are not too young to know or seek the purpose of God for your life. God is not a respecter of persons. It doesn't matter how old you are now, you can still know the purpose of God for your life. The teenage and youth years should be a good time to begin to seek after God's purpose for your life. Seek the Lord now while you are still young and strong. God is willing to reveal it to you, so you may walk in it.

Do you know that each day that passes is a day wasted if you are not walking in your purpose? And that only you can walk in your gifting and purpose! Friend, do not allow anyone despise your youth. If you know the gifting God has placed in you, go ahead and begin to walk in it. Suffice to say however, that you cannot decide your purpose, but you can discover it. God had established it long before you were ever born.

For I know the thoughts and plans that I have for you, says the Lord, thoughts and plans for welfare and peace and not for evil, to give you hope in your final outcome. Jeremiah 29:11

God has invested so much in you.

Friend, you are loaded with great gifting and talents; with great ambitions and destiny. God has invested so much in you. He has put a gifting and ability in you for a specific job but He will not do the job for you. You are to do it yourself. You have to find your gift and develop it. You are too gifted to waste your life doing nothing with it. You see, the gifts and calling God gave to you are with you whether you use it or not. Inside every one of us is a gift. Your gifting is what would make the world know who you are and know God.

For God's gifts and calling are irrevocable. [He never withdraws them when once they are given, and He does not change His mind about those to whom He gives His grace or to whom He sends His call.] Romans 11:29

In other words, God never withdraws the gifts He puts in you, even if you turn away from Him; His calling and gifting remains. How amazing! He put it in you to use for the edification of the Body of Christ and to give Him glory. Please get a grip on your purpose.

Receiving a gift is like getting a rare gemstone; anyway you look at it, you see beauty refracted. Proverbs 17:8 (the message)

In other words, your education and God given gifting are not the same. If you will use your God given giftedness, you will prosper beyond your wildest imagination. That is why the devil is trying so hard to stop you from recognising and knowing the purpose of God for your life, let alone fulfil your destiny. Don't sit on your gifts, it is your endowment.

How do I know my purpose?

How will I get to know my purpose? You may ask. You see friend, God created you and I first and foremost to have fellowship with Him, to commune with Him and have a relationship with Him through His Son Jesus and until you come to have that beautiful intimate relationship with Him, you may never discover or understand His purpose for your life. How do I have fellowship with God? You may ask. How do you have fellowship with a dear close friend? By spending time together, talking and sharing. In other words, you can have fellowship with God by spending quality time in the Word, in prayer, praise and worship and being silent before Him so He can talk to you.

Go into His presence with an expectant heart to hear from Him. You may plan your time with Him and the place of meeting with Him. And as you consistently keep doing these, your relationship begins to grow and grow and real soon, you will begin to hear Him speak not just to you, but with you regularly. You need to invest time in your relationship with God, the same way you would take the time and plan your relationship with your best friend. The Bible says that when you draw close to Him, He will draw close to you. Start today, to develop your relationship with God. Being in His presence is having the consciousness that He is always with you wherever you are and whenever you speak to Him.

Ask Him for the wisdom to discern His will and purpose for your life.

Delight yourself also in the Lord, and He will give you the desires and secret petitions of your heart. Proverbs 37:4 God will lead you and direct you as you diligently seek Him and His will for your life. See Proverbs 37:23.

Your gifting is not for you alone

The purpose of God upon your life, and the gifting and talent, even that special grace, is not really for you or about you. It is for someone else, it is about all of the people that are supposed to be blessed by your gifting. God wants you to use all of it and all of the opportunities to benefit the world. Knowing that the gifting God has given you is not for you should put some 'holy fear' in you, knowing that you will stand before God some day and give account to Him as to what you did with it.

As each of you has received a gift (a particular spiritual talent, a gracious divine endowment), employ it for one another as [befits] good trustees of God's many-sided grace [faithful stewards of the extremely diverse powers and gifts granted to Christians by unmerited favour]. 1 Peter 4:10

God has given you the responsibility of ministering in His Name until He returns. You are His bill board and His mouth piece to share the Good News to the world. You are God's ambassadors. Paul understood this so well when he said:

But my life is worth nothing to me unless I use it for finishing the work assigned me by the Lord Jesus – the work of telling others the Good News about the wonderful grace of God. Acts 20:24 (NLT)

Friend, it is so amazing to know that God has called you and chosen you to share the Good News to the world. It is a task that must be done. Now you certainly do not have to be a pastor before you can share the Good News; you don't have to be a leader in the church before you can do that, and that's why God put that gifting in you. If you will recognise and know your gifting, you will do great and awesome things for God. Start with sharing with your peers in school, at the sports centre and wherever.

Come let us tell of the Lord's greatness; let us exalt His Name together. Psalm 34:3 (NLT)

Discover your gifting

What is that idea or thing that stirs you up whenever you think about it? Could it be that God put it there in you to use for His glory or could it be that God put it in your heart to do something about it? I encourage you to take some time and look into your heart. Think on that thing or those things that when you imagine doing brings joy and fulfilment to you. Think on the great impact it will have on the lives that you touch. Use that gifting or talent in you now. Don't let it waste. Somebody once said that the only thing worse than death is life without purpose. See Ecclesiastes 2:4-11

For what will it profit a man if he gains the whole world and forfeits his life [his blessed life in the Kingdom of God]? Or what would a man give as an exchange for his [blessed] life [in the Kingdom of God]? Matthew 16:26

Friend, God has given you a unique gifting to use and fulfil your purpose. Know your gifting and purpose and begin to walk in it. It doesn't matter how people may see you or perceive you. This does not change your uniqueness. Forget yesterday and celebrate your uniqueness today. Be all that God has called you to be and to do. Remain in your own lane. Do not pursue or run with someone else's purpose, calling or gifting. Do not follow the crowd. Can a man run a race to completion and the prize be given to someone else? But whoever runs the race and finishes wins the price.

David knew his area of gifting, and strengths. He understood it and took advantage of it. David had knowledge and experience of his strength; he knew how to use the stone and the fling. He had tested his gifting and used it to the fullest and glorified God with it. The Bible says that David had courage and was fearless. Find your gifting, study it and grow in it and do not run in other people's strength. It will cause you to be courageous and fearless.

Then Saul gave David his own armour – a bronze helmet and a coat of mail. David put it on, strapped the sword over it, and took a step or two to see what it was like, for he had never worn such things before. "I can't go in these" he protested to Saul. I'm not used to them." So David took them off again. He picked up five smooth stones from a stream and put them into his shepherd's bag. Then, armed only with his shepherd's staff and sling, he started across the valley to fight the Philistine. 1 Samuel 17:38-40 (NLT)

You see, David could not use King Saul's armour because that was not in him. It was for King Saul. How many times have you tried to copy somebody else's gifting or purpose? You need to be comfortable with whom you are, with the particular grace, talents or gifting that God has put in you. For only then will you be able to make a difference and shine! Learn to celebrate your gifting for that's what makes you so different and unique. David defeated Goliath because he stayed in the area of his gifting which God used. You will only prosper in the area of your gifting! Stay on your lane. You can be very busy for the Lord, but if you are not walking in the area of your purpose and call, you may be wasting precious time. Do you know that you can be busy but not effective? This is true when you are walking and working, but not in the area of your gifting and purpose.

Samuel even at such a young age of twelve years old understood his purpose and walked in it. The Bible records that God did not allow his word fall to the ground. In other words, God backed every word Samuel spoke to the people of Israel throughout his time and reign as a prophet. Joseph understood his purpose and walked in his gifting and was able to fulfil the purpose of God for his life and God honoured him.

You could face opposition when you are walking in your purpose, even from people you never imagined. But stay focused and remain in it. God will not allow you to go through what you are not able to handle. Joseph faced oppositions but he remained focused. David faced oppositions but he didn't allow himself to give in to it. He who has started the good work in you is faithful to complete it. If He gave you the gift, if He gave you the talent and called you into that purpose, He will give you the grace to stand and over come every opposition.

Friend, make the choice today to begin to walk in the consciousness of your purpose. It's never too late to discover your purpose and walk in it. There is what the Word calls redeeming the time!

Remember:

- You were created and placed on the earth by God for a purpose
- It has been said that the only thing worse than death is life without purpose
- True success in life is knowing your purpose and fulfilling it
- Do you know that the best way to waste your time is to not know your purpose; that you can be very busy but not effective?
- You cannot determine your purpose but you discover it
- Your gifting, talents and anointing is not for you but for someone else
- That the gifts and callings God gave you are with you whether you use it or not. However, that you will give account to God of every gift and talent you did not use here on earth.

Think on these:

But my life is worth nothing to me unless I use it for finishing the work assigned me by the Lord Jesus – the work of telling others the Good News about the wonderful grace of God. Acts 20:24 (NLT)

Your thoughts:

Study Questions

1. Do you know your purpose in life, and what are you doing about it?

----

2. Do you know or have you recognised your God given gifting and calling upon your life? Write them down

----

----

3. What is that desire, idea or thing that stirs you up when you think about it or them?

----

4. Are you comfortable with who you are?

----

5. What is purpose?

Principle #8
Discipline – Break Those Barriers!

Discipline has been defined as that determined effort on our part that corrects moulds and perfects the character of a person. Someone once said that, a professional athlete will invest countless hours into practicing and training. He will stretch his abilities farther and farther each year, learning new plays and tactics and will only allow foods into his body that build, cleanse and strengthen. He will condition his mind to know every play until he can do them in his sleep. He will condition his body so that he executes each play with effortless grace. When he reaches this level, the opposing team finds it almost impossible to stop him.

A lot of people recognize a champion only when he steps up the podium. However, he actually had already become a champion far before it. In fact, he had become a champion many years before that glorious moment. This is as a result of the fact that, to reach that moment, first and foremost, he has to become a champion in his daily life. He has to train hard for years, control his diet, and deny a lot of pleasures to prepare for the contests. While other people choose to live whatever way they want, he chooses to live a disciplined life. Most people only see him in the glorious moment, but it is this lifestyle of discipline that actually brings him to the podium.

Dear friend, making the choice to live a disciplined life is a decision that you must make for yourself. The discipline I am speaking to you about is more than just about good ethics such as, having a special diet to lose some weight, doing some exercises to keep fit, quitting smoking, drugs or alcohol. It's not just about completing a long list of do's and don'ts, or being ethically right. It's not just about making

New Year resolutions and then forgetting it as the year progresses, and all of these are good. However, the discipline I am talking about is submitting to God, submitting to His Word!

John 8:31-32 says, if you abide in my Word [hold fast to my teachings and live in accordance with them], you are truly my disciples. And you shall know the Truth and the Truth will set you free.

It is the truth that you know, that can set you free. If you cannot be disciplined enough to submit to God's Word, you cannot be disciplined enough to achieve any good thing and be a success in life period! To be a successful teenager, youth, young man or woman, you must make the conscious decision to live a life of discipline. Discipline is the ability to stick to actions, thoughts and behaviour that ultimately leads to improvement and success.

Discipline will restore order into your life. There is a sense of freedom, peace and fulfilment that comes with living a life of discipline. Suffice to say that, it cannot be accomplished by anyone else but you. You have to want it, desire it, seek after it and you will have it. This discipline involves self restraint, courage and perseverance. It requires self control and the more self control you exercise or practice; the easier it will be to live a disciplined life. You can achieve this if you set your mind and heart to it.

What are your dreams and aspirations? What do you want to accomplish, who do you want to become in life? God has called you to do mighty things for Him. He has called you into greatness and has put some awesome gifts in you but it would only take discipline to bring this into fulfilment. God has given us a spirit of discipline.

2 Timothy 1:7 says, for God did not give us a spirit of timidity (of cowardice, of craven and cringing and fawning fear), but [He has given us a spirit] of power and of love and of calm and well balanced mind and discipline and self control. (See also Galatians 5:22-23).

Someone once said that discipline is what we need the most in our lives but want the least. This is so very true. We all want the best in life, we want to be successful, but when it comes to paying the price for this, and doing all we need to do to achieve this, guess what? We become lazy and postpone it to tomorrow. Sadly, tomorrow never comes. I have come to realise that so much of the lack of rest, stability and consistency in our lives can be traced to a lack of discipline. Yes, there may be other causes, but surely a lack of discipline is at the top of the list. No matter how gifted or talented you are, in order to fulfil God's perfect will in your life, you must make the choice to live a consistent life of discipline.

Proverbs 24:10 says, if you faint in the day of adversity, your strength is small.

Days of adversity will come to all of us, but it's only by living a consistent, life of discipline that the strength of character can be developed in us, which would enable us to face those days of adversity without us fainting. A consistent work for God can be done only by those who have learnt to be disciplined and work even when they 'don't feel like it'. It has been said that the evidence of a man with a disciplined life will be seen not only in greater spirituality, but also in greater efficiency and effectiveness in everything that he does for God. This will show up in many ordinary matters of your daily life. A story was told of a research test.

The Research – What a result!

"During the 1960s, psychologist Walter Mischel conducted what became known as "the marshmallow test" with four year olds in the preschool at Stanford University. The object of the exercise was to assess each preschool's ability to delay gratification. Each child was given one marshmallow. They were told that they could eat it immediately or, if they waited until the researcher returned in 20 minutes, they could have two marshmallows. Some kids in the group just couldn't wait. They gobbled down the marshmallow immediately. The rest struggled hard to resist eating it. They covered their eyes, talked to themselves, sang, played games, even tried to go to sleep. The preschoolers who were able to wait were rewarded with two marshmallows when the researcher returned. Twelve fourteen years later the same kids were re-evaluated. The differences were astonishing. Those who had been able to control their impulses and delay gratification as four year olds were more effective socially and personally as teenagers. They had higher levels of assertiveness, self confidence, trustworthiness, dependability and a superior ability to control stress. Remarkably, their Scholastic Aptitude Test (SAT) scores were also 210 points higher than the 'instant gratification group!"

Dear friend, you cannot reach your full maturity or potential in anything you do without living a daily life of discipline. **1 Corinthians 9:27 says, but [like a boxer] I buffet my body [handle it roughly, discipline it by hardships] and subdue it, for fear that after proclaiming to others the Gospel and things pertaining to it, I myself should become unfit [not stand the test, be unapproved and rejected as a counterfeit].** The Living translation says, 'like an athlete, I punish my body, treating it roughly, training it to do what it should and not what it wants to...'

A lack of discipline will cause you to be unproductive. **Proverbs 20:4 says that the sluggard does not plow when winter sets in; therefore he begs in harvest and has nothing.**

You need to be disciplined enough to subordinate less important things to the more important ones. You must therefore learn to give first priority to the Kingdom of God and His righteousness in your practical daily life. This would require the discipline to reject day by day, that great list of activities that clamour for your attention and time but that would hinder the doing of more important things such as, spending time with God, His Word and in prayer.

Discipline in this area will push you to stand up, turn off the TV and go pray when it is time, push you out of bed early in the morning to seek God instead of rolling around for another half an hour, while still wide awake, push you to go out of your house when it's raining or snowing in order to attend a church service. Learning how to prioritize your activities and sticking to a schedule will help you. Remember, we only have 24 hours in a day. Accomplish something worthwhile each day. Discipline requires a willingness to stand and not quit in the face of adversity. You need to be disciplined in selecting your priorities.

Are you submitting to the Word of God? The grace of God is available for you. **Hebrew 12:1 says, therefore then, since we are surrounded by so great a cloud of witnesses [who have borne testimony to the truth], let us strip off and throw aside every encumbrance (unnecessary weight) and that sin which so readily (deftly and cleverly) clings to and entangles us, and let us run with patient endurance and steady and active persistence the appointed course of the race that is set before us.**

The Race for life – You must win

There is a race marked out for us. It is a race you and I must run and it is a race we must win. It is a race for life even eternal life. Dear friend, when you are involved in a race for life, you cannot afford to be hindered, to get entangled in anything that would stop you or slow you down from finishing that race. You must run the race not just to be a participant but you must run the race to win.

1 Corinthians 9:24 says, do you not know that in a race all the runners compete, but [only] one receives the prize? So run [your race] that you may lay hold [of the prize] and make it yours. Please read 2 Timothy 2:4-5 says no soldier when in service gets entangled in the enterprises of [civilian] life; his aim is to satisfy and please the one who enlisted him. And if anyone enters competitive games, he is not crowned unless he competes lawfully (fairly, according to the rules laid down). See also 2 Timothy 4:7-8.

You and I must run this race to finish. It's a race of endurance, for there are no short cuts and it's a race where you and I cannot afford to look back. You must keep your eyes on the goal. Please read Hebrews 5:12-14 and Mark 4:13-20. If you must win this race, you need to be disciplined. What is that dream, vision or desire of yours? What has God called you to do? Are you working in it, working towards it or have you given up on it or about to, due to circumstances around you. Hold on to your dreams, don't quit, and don't throw in the towel. It's not over until God says it's over and that means it's not over until you win!

Be encouraged my dear friend. Be strong and make the decision today to start afresh with living a life of discipline. Choose to be disciplined enough to start it and finish it.

Philippians 3:13-14 says, I do not consider, brethren, that I have captured and made it my own [yet]; but one thing I do [it is my one aspiration]: forgetting what lies behind and straining forward to what lies ahead, I press on toward the goal to win the [supreme and heavenly] prize to which God in Christ Jesus is calling us upward.

So many people who had great visions, dreams, gifting and calling from God have gotten distracted along the way and could therefore not fulfil their purpose and destiny. You must understand that it is the devils plan to stop you from fulfilling your purpose in God. It is his plan to stop you from enjoying that good wonderful life full of blessings and abundance that God wants you to live and enjoy.

Jesus said, "No procrastination. No backward looks. You can't put God's Kingdom off till tomorrow. Seize the day." Luke 9:62 (the message)

One of the ways the devil is doing this is by causing the children of God to become lazy and slothful in the things of God, even in fulfilling their God given dreams, their purpose and destiny. You must be careful not to get distracted along the way in this race for life that we all are in.

Discipline requires Commitment

It takes discipline to achieve the things of God. And this starts with your daily routines, your habits. Discipline will help you to remain focused on the things that God has called you to do, on your dreams and aspirations, your vision.

You must be careful not to get distracted along the way in this race for life that we all are in. **Jeremiah 29:11 says, for I know the thoughts and plans that I have for you, says the Lord, thoughts and plans for welfare and peace and not for evil, to give you hope in your final outcome.**

If you are to see this scripture come to pass in your life, you must make the choice to begin to live a life of discipline. For God's standard requires it. In other words, if you are to see the manifestation of God's promises in your life, you have to go the extra mile with Him, for God requires an extra level of commitment and this can only be achieved through discipline. Discipline is hard work but it's worth every effort. This discipline will help you to get more out of yourself and will enable you to give your best towards your endeavours. Discipline is a vital key to success.

Dear friend, living a life of discipline is so, so important. It is this discipline that will bring your gifting to their highest level of effectiveness. Let's look at the story of David. David's first victory was not over Goliath. You see, his life of discipline with years of practice as a shepherd boy watching over his sheep, defending them against wild animals such as a lion and a bear had prepared him for that moment and season. It had equipped him and given him the spirit and skill needed to take on the philistine champion Goliath. Please read 1 Samuel 17:34-51.

"David said, I've been a shepherd, tending sheep for my father. Whenever a lion or bear came and took a lamb from the flock, I'd go after it, knock it down, and rescue the lamb. If it turned on me, I'd grab it by the throat, wring its neck, and kill it. Lion or bear, it made no difference – I killed it. And I'll do the same to this Philistine pig who is taunting the troops of God – Alive. God, who delivered me from the teeth of the lion and the claws of the bear, will deliver me from this Philistine" 1 Samuel 17:34-37 (the message)

It was that same life of discipline that saw him through the rough times he went through being a slave boy, out of Potiphar's wife's trap and lust for him. It was that same life of discipline that also caused Joseph to become so effective that he was promoted to be next in command to Pharaoh in Egypt. Please read Genesis 39:1-23; 41:39-46

Discipline will strengthen your will. Discipline doesn't make you rigid, but it makes you resilient. This was the case for Shadrach, Meshach and Abednego, who refused to bow to the king's idol, even when they were threatened with being put into the fiery burning furnace. Daniel 3:17-18.

Shedrach, Meshach, and Abednego answered King Nebuchadnezza, "your threat means nothing to us. If you throw us in the fire, the God we serve can rescue us from your roaring furnace and anything else you might cook up, o king. But even if He doesn't, it wouldn't make a bit of difference, o king. We still wouldn't serve your gods or worship the gold statue you set up" (the message)

They had all been toughened through discipline, in order to face such a great test. How disciplined are you to look at a seemingly seducing temptation or adversity in the eye, and say, 'I will not compromise my faith in God, no matter what!' We must cultivate a life of discipline that will toughen us too, so that when we go through challenges, which will always come, we will be strong knowing in whom we have believed and stand firm and not quit in spite of the adversity. A key difference between successful people and leaders, who have gone through rough and tough times and made it to the top, was as a result of a lifestyle of self discipline.

What weight is holding you down? Get rid of it!

Someone once said that, the nature of people is always the same; that it is their habits that separate them. What weight is holding you back? What habit is keeping you in bondage? Could it be a lack of discipline? When you give yourself to the things of the flesh, you cut yourself away from God's direction in your life. Sow to your spirit and experience God's hand and grace upon your life. Only then can you produce good fruit for the Lord.

John 15:8 says 'when you bear (produce) much fruit, my father is honoured and glorified, and you show and prove yourselves to be true followers of mine'.

It takes discipline to bear fruit. Make the choice today to begin to live a life of discipline. Jesus is our greatest and perfect example! He lived a consistent life of discipline. Matthew 16:24, Then Jesus said to His disciples, if anyone desires to be my disciple, let him deny himself [disregard, lose sight of, and forget himself and his own interests] and take up his cross and follow me [cleave steadfastly to me, conform wholly to my example in living and, if need be, in dying, also].

Hebrews 12:2 (the message) says,

Keep your eyes on Jesus, who both began and finished this race we're in. Study how He did it; because He never lost sight of where He was headed – that exhilarating finish in and with God; He could put up with anything along the way: cross, shame, whatever. And now He's there, in the place of honour, right alongside God. When you find yourselves flagging in your *faith, go* over that story again, item by item, that long litany of hostility He plowed through. That will shoot adrenaline into your souls!

How disciplined are you with your studies? Do you just pick up your books just days before your exams, or are you disciplined enough to follow up with your studies even when you know your exams are still far away. God desires excellence from you in the area of your academic work too you know. How disciplined are you at work, with your job? Do you always work as though you were being paid a million pounds per annum? The Word of God says that we should do our jobs as unto Him. Guess what? God's reward to you would be more than a million pounds!

How disciplined are you at home? You know what you do at home I don't. But remember, knowing what is right to do and not doing it, is a sin. Be a blessing at your home and to your family and household. What about your career or business? Are you disciplined enough to follow it through and pursue it passionately to become a success? How disciplined are you with money? Do you spend and buy stuff just to impress people? Can you afford to buy what you are paying for with your credit card? I encourage you to spend wisely.

How disciplined are you with your ministry, call or gifting upon your life? Remember the story of the Talents. Don't waste your talent or gifting, for you will give account of how you used it to God. God put it in you for His glory, for you to shine with it so you can attract the world to God through it. You are the light of the world. Use your gifts;

use that talent that God has given to you. Be disciplined enough to develop yourself in that area and use it to the glory of God. Invest time in the area of your call or gifting. God believes in you! What decisions have you been postponing that you know you should make now or supposed to have made? What have you been putting off? Procrastination is a thief, do not allow it into your life or it will steal your future and destiny.

Are you disciplined in your relationship with God? Is God number one on your list of priorities? Or did you put Him at the bottom of the list. Oh! Wait a minute; He is not even on the list! Friend, God wants to talk to you and with you. He wants to spend time with you and tell you awesome things and show you great things concerning you; He wants you to have the best and be the best and He is not too busy to spend time with you. Don't be too busy or too lazy to spend time with Him. You can do nothing without Him! Dare to be disciplined to put Him first in everything you do in your life!

Always look at the bigger picture

Make the choice today to create a great future for yourself. It has been said that you are the prophet of your own life. You can make a difference and be the difference in the world. Remember and never ever forget that great accomplishment requires discipline. Dare to shine! You all know or have heard about the story of Esau and Jacob in **Genesis 25:29-34**

Jacob was boiling pottage (lentil stew) one day. When Esau came from the field and was faint [with hunger]. And Esau said to Jacob, I beg you, let me have some of that red lentil stew to eat, for I am faint and famished! That is why his name was called Edom [red]. Jacob answered, then sell me today your birthright (the rights of a firstborn). Esau said, see here, I am at the point of death; what good can this birthright do me? Jacob said, swear to me today [that you are selling it to me]; and he swore to [Jacob] and sold him his birthright. Then Jacob gave Esau bread and stew of lentils, and he ate and drank and rose up and went his way. Thus Esau scorned his birthright as beneath his notice.

Oh my God, how terrible! How could somebody sell his birthright for a bowl of stew? You see, Esau knew he was his father's favourite son. However, he did not take the birthright seriously for whatever reason. A lack of discipline is definitely one of the major reasons. Friend, what has God called you to do or what gifts has He put in you that you are not taking seriously for whatever reason. Jacob was ready to give away his soup and make another one later. He must have been hungry to have prepared the soup in the first place, but he was prepared to sacrifice it for something better.

Not so for his brother Esau. He was not prepared to wait; he lacked the discipline to persevere; he wanted instant gratification for something less important. He was willing to sacrifice his future blessing for a bowl of soup! It takes only discipline to give up instant pleasure and satisfaction for a higher and better goal. Watch out for the Esau syndrome; trading away the great gifting and Talent that God has given you to use for His glory just to satisfy a short – term appetite. As you very well know, Esau later regretted his actions and wanted to have his blessing back but it was too late!

Discipline will enable you to accomplish all of those things, dreams and vision you have always wanted to do, but for whatever reason, never got to doing them. It is a success skill that you must develop. It is focusing your full attention on whatever you are doing that you want to be good at and not being distracted by what other people are doing. The choices you make today, would determine your tomorrow. Always look at the bigger picture! Whenever you find yourself desiring to satisfy an immediate need, stop and think about the consequences of that choice or action. You can live a life of discipline but it is a choice only you can make and follow through. Be the difference in the world, make a difference. Dare to shine!

Remember:

- If you cannot be disciplined enough to submit to God's Word, you cannot be disciplined enough to achieve any good thing and be a success in life period!

- A key difference between successful people and leaders, who have gone through rough and tough times and made it to the top, was as a result of a lifestyle of self discipline.

- Dear friend, you cannot reach your full maturity or potential in anything you do without living a daily life of discipline.

- It takes only discipline to give up instant pleasure and satisfaction for a higher and better goal.

- Someone once said that, the nature of people is always the same; that it is their habits that separate them.

- It takes discipline to bear fruit.

Think on these:

So many people who had great visions, dreams, gifting and calling from God have gotten distracted along the way and could therefore not fulfil their purpose and destiny, because of a lack of discipline.

Your thoughts:

Study Questions

1. What do you understand by the Word Discipline?

----

2. What areas in your life do you think you lack discipline?

----

3. What are your plans in dealing with them?

----

4. What does the Bible say about the issue of discipline or a lack of it?

----

5. Are you a disciplined person?

Principle #9

Obedience: A Master Key to a Successful Life!

"You shall walk after the Lord your God and [reverently] fear Him, and keep His commandments and obey His voice, and you shall serve Him and cling to Him. Deuteronomy 13:4 ...that you may OBEY HIS VOICE, and that you may cling to Him, for He is your life and the length of your days..." Deuteronomy 30:19

"If they OBEY and SERVE HIM, they shall spend their days in prosperity, and their years in pleasantness and joy" Job 36:11

We are in a day and age where our teenagers and youths, young men and women including Christians just like to hear the Word of God, but do not like to do what they hear and what the Word says; A generation of people who have a laid back attitude concerning the Word of God and the things of God; a people who just do not take God seriously, who ask why they should believe in a God they cannot see. Hello! Obeying God's Word should be your top priority!

If anyone hears my teachings and fails to observe them [does not keep them, but disregards them], it is not I who judges him. For I have not come to judge and to condemn and to pass sentence and to inflict penalty on the world, but to save the world. Anyone who rejects me and persistently sets me at naught, refusing to accept my teachings, has his judge [however]; for the [very] message that I have spoken will itself judge and convict him at the last day. John 12:47-48

You see, the teenage and youth years should be a time to enjoy life, but it is also a very crucial time when you have to decide the direction or path your life will take. The question is will the direction or path you choose ultimately lead you to a life of joy, happiness and a productive life? Or will it lead you into one of fear, depression, unhappiness and failure both now and in the future? Remember, your future success and happiness will depend on the choices you make in your teen or youth years.

Honour and enjoy your creator while you're still young, before the years take their toll and your vigor wanes, before your vision dims and the world blurs and the winter years keep you close to the fire. Ecclesiastes 12:1(the message)

Therefore remove [the lusts that end in] sorrow and vexation from your heart and mind and put away evil from your body, for youth and the dawn of life are vanity [transitory, idle, empty, and devoid of truth]. Ecclesiastes 11:10

There is a way which seems right to a man and appears straight before him, but at the end of it is the way of death. Proverbs 14:12

Even as a teenager or youth, God has a great plan and purpose for your life, and He wants to make your name great on the earth. He has great and awesome promises for you through His Word and God wants you to spend your days in prosperity and your years in pleasures. However, all of these are dependent upon your making the choice to live a life of obedience to Him, to His Word! God has given you the free will to live your life the way you want. He has given you the ability to make your own decisions, to obey Him or to live your life outside of Him, His Word. He will never force you to do anything or go against your will, but it is His desire that you seek after Him, and after His Word and counsel. Remember the song "trust and obey for there's no other way to be happy in Jesus, but to trust and obey"

What is obedience?

The dictionary definition of obedience is: dutifully complying with the commands or instructions of those in authority; submissive behaviour with respect to another person; the trait of being willing to obey.

Based on the above, from the Christian view point, obedience is dutifully complying with the commands and instructions of God and His Word; it is willingly submitting yourself and your will to Him and His Word for your life. Anything contrary to the above is disobedience; it is failing to follow and do God's Word. God requires for you to live a consistent life of obedience to Him. If you want to have a beautiful intimate relationship with God and see His great and awesome promises made manifest in your life, you must make the choice to live a life of continuous obedience to God. If you resign yourself to partially obeying God, you will limit your spiritual growth and fail to receive all of the blessings and goodness of God for your life.

Are you living a life of obedience to God? Are you living according to the standards of God's Word? You see, the choice of obedience will lead you into a life of blessings and the choice of disobedience will lead you into a life of curses, problems and even death. Disobedience is at the root of all sin and it is the cause of all problems. In other words, your obedience is what will give birth to the blessings of God upon your life here on earth. However, the obedience God demands from you as His child is an obedience that flows from a willing heart and not just something you do because you have to. Obedience is an attitude, and one that God desires and expects from His children. This is because, you could appear on the outside to be obedient but in reality, you are rebelling inside.

Half obedience is disobedience

God is not interested in you being half obedient or being grudgingly obedient. He wants your full obedience. Remember, partial obedience is disobedience before God. You see, God does not tolerate disobedience neither is He prepared to negotiate with it. He however shows mercy to the disobedient who repents but how many of you know that His Spirit will not always strive with men. It is not the hearers that succeed and make it to the top in life, it is the doers yes, the obedient!

"If you are willing and obedient, you shall eat the good of the land". Isaiah 1:19

Being obedient to God is not the same as sticking to the speed limit so you don't get a ticket or fine if you disobeyed. Obedience to God is living Gods Word because you want to, because of your love for Him. It involves a willingness to always want to do what God says, in His Word. It is not dependent on how you feel, think, or what you see or what people say; but a willingness to do what the Word of God says, no matter what. It is doing the right thing no matter the pressure around you or on you. For only then will you eat the good of the land! Obedience is the mark of the spirit filled life, a characteristic of those that love God. It is the mark of a true Christian!

"Now that you've cleaned up your lives by following the truth, love one another as if your lives depended on it. Your new life is not like your old life. Your old birth came from mortal sperm; your new birth comes from God's living Word. Just think: a life conceived by God Himself! 1 Peter 1:22 (the message)

[Live] as children of obedience [to God]; do not conform yourselves to the evil desires [that governed you] in your former ignorance [when you did not know the requirements of the Gospel]. But as the One who called you is holy, you yourselves also be holy in all your conduct and manner of living." 1 Peter1:14-15

God's Word demands that you reject your former negative lifestyle and way of living and be obedient to Him, and His Word. He demands that you have a pure heart before Him and before men, a heart focused on Him, knowing Him, having an understanding of His Will and obeying Him completely. However, these can only be developed in you where there is obedience and a clear conscience before God and men.

Obedience - an absolute must have in today's world

The issue of obedience to God is so relevant today and now, especially in a time and age as these, where teenagers, youths, young men and women of all ages are being bombarded with peer pressure to follow the crowd, seeking after fleeting pleasures that are but temporal and will not and cannot bring any lasting happiness to them; making wrong choices that end up damaging their bodies, self worth and ultimately destroying their lives. A time and age where teenagers and youths are suffering and dying from the effects of alcohol, tobacco, drugs and harmful substances to achieve a 'high' and engaging in illicit sex which has now become a common thing among them; disobeying the law and damning the consequences.

Sadly, a lot of Christian teenagers, youth, young men and women are falling into the temptation and urge to follow after them, their peers, friends and people who are not Christians, who do not understand what it means to live a life of holiness unto God; a people who do not understand Covenant with God. You all are familiar with the story of King Saul and the instructions God gave Him, which was to destroy Amalek and everything in it and not spare any; and how Saul spared Agag and the best of the sheep, oxen, fatlings, lambs and all that were good; which was against Gods instruction to him to destroy everything and not spare!

"Then Samuel said, do you think all GOD wants are sacrifices empty rituals just for show? He wants you to listen to him! Plain listening is the thing, not staging a lavish religious production. Not doing what GOD tells you is far worse than fooling around in the occult. Getting self – important around GOD is far worse than making deals with your dead ancestors. Because you said No to GOD'S command, He says No to your kingship. Saul gave in and confessed, "I've sinned. I've trampled roughshod over GOD'S Word and your instructions. I cared more about pleasing the people. I let them tell me what to do. Oh, absolve me of my sin!" 1 Samuel 15:22-24, (the message)

You see, although Saul succeeded in the battle, he thought he could do what he wanted, what he thought was best according to his standards and not according to Gods specific instructions. And although his motive may have been probably reasonable before men, God saw his decision and action as disobedience. God told him through His prophet Samuel, that He (God) required obedience and not sacrifice. God says that disobedience is rebellion and stubbornness against Him; it is as bad as Witchcraft. This is definitely a startling comparison and shows how much God hates disobedience.

Catch the Foxes

Friend, do you realise that each day a teenager, young man or woman is being hurt, injured, put in jail and even killed as a result of disobedience? Following the wrong friends and wrong crowd, putting their own lives in danger just to please someone! Do you know that even the small decisions you make can sometimes bring about the greatest consequences? Hanging out with the wrong person/people, telling a 'little lie', trying that drug or alcohol or cigarette you know you shouldn't even consider trying or taking, following your friends to that club you know isn't a good idea etc friend, you must realise that it's the little foxes that spoil the vine.

Those little things that you keep doing contrary to God's Word and Will for your life. You need to CATCH the FOXES and destroy them before they destroy your future! This is so sad but so true of our teenagers today, including our Christian teenagers and youth, who already know the Lord. Would you listen and obey the voice of your friends rather than listening and obeying the voice of God? Just because you think your friends or peers are cool and you want to belong in their clique? You cannot say that you know God or have a relationship with Him and yet trample on His Word by not doing what He says. Remember, the choices you make today will determine tomorrow's effects!

You were running the race nobly. Who has interfered in (hindered and stopped you from) your heeding and following the truth? Galatians 5:7

Disobedience always comes with a price just as obedience comes with a price too. Saul's disobedience cost him his throne. Moses' disobedience in misrepresenting God before the people cost him not entering the Promised Land. Samson's disobedience cost him his eyes and his life. God desires that you represent Him as He truly is.

"And the Lord said to Moses and Aaron, because you did not believe in (rely on, cling to) me to sanctify me in the eyes of the Israelites, you therefore shall not bring this congregation into the land which I have given them." Numbers 20:12

Notice, that they were both under pressure because of the people. Nevertheless, God still held them responsible for their actions for not obeying Him. Friend, God cares about you and wants the best for you, but you cannot afford to disobey Him because of anyone or anything in your life. Nothing is worth disobeying God for. Whatever challenge you are going through right now, is just temporal. You will come out of it in victory if you will remain obedient to God's Word even regarding that situation! Adam and Eve disobeyed God's instruction to them in the Garden of Eden and were driven out of the Garden of Eden, which brought them hardship and made their lives difficult and burdensome, coupled with sorrow. What a terrible price to pay for their disobedience. Obedience is so very important, whether you understand God's purpose for your life or not. God demands total obedience to Him. Who is influencing you right now? Whose words are you obeying? Remember what we spoke about regarding friendship!

Secrets of Obedience

How obedient are you in prayer? How obedient are you to your parents and to authority? Can you be obedient to the Word of God? Walking in obedience would require you to regularly study the Word and have daily fellowship with God. However, you must take those same Words into your heart and DO what it says! Remember, the Word of God says that not doing what is right to do is a sin before God. God has given you and me awesome and great promises in His Word but how would you know these promises and appropriate them into your life if you do not study the Word. It is your responsibility and no one else's.

This Book of the law shall not depart out of your mouth, but you shall meditate on it day and night, that you may observe and do according to all that is written in it. For then you shall make your way prosperous, and then you shall deal wisely and have good success. Joshua 1:8

Do you take the time to daily study the Word of God? If you are not obedient with the written Word of God, how can you be obedient with the spoken Word? It is my submission that, if you cannot be obedient to the written Word of God (The Bible) to study it, and do what God commands, you will not be able to hear the spoken Word from God. For you are not obedient with the written one. Tell me, if you cannot be faithful and obedient to diligently study the written Word that you can see and touch, how on earth will you be faithful and obedient to hear and do what God reveals to you by His spoken Word, knowing that you cannot see or touch God as it were? You see, obedience will bring you good success and when you are obedient, the blessing of God will come upon you and flow in your life. You need to look for opportunities to be obedient to God.

He who is faithful in a very little [thing] is faithful also in much, and he who is dishonest and unjust in a very little [thing] is dishonest and unjust also in much. Luke 16:10

And he said to him, well done, excellent bond servant! Because you have been faithful and trustworthy in a very little [thing], you shall have authority over ten cities. Luke 19:17

Can you be faithful?

God demands that you be faithful in the little things. Will God find you faithful to His Word? You see obedience and faithfulness go hand in hand. In other words, they go together and are inseparable. The issue of obedience and faithfulness will determine what you can accomplish and how far you will go in life. Real Bible worship is obedience to God. In other words, you cannot worship God without obedience, because worship comes together with obedience. Jesus said,

If you [really] love me, you will keep (obey) my commands. John 14:15

Friend, you cannot obey God or be obedient to Him, and His Word if you do not have a relationship with God, you cannot shine and make a difference in your generation without obedience to God's Word. What kind of relationship do you have with God? Is it an outer court relationship? One that only starts and ends in the church? Is it a sugar daddy type of relationship where you come to God only when you have a need and when it's met, you go off and never return until the next time you have another need? God desires for you to have an intimate relationship with Him. He wants to spend time with you and talk to you. He wants to enjoy fellowship with you. Yes, YOU! You have to realise that every relationship needs fellowship to grow. Learn to spend time with God. He is eagerly waiting for you each day.

It's not always easy sometimes to be obedient, because, your flesh wants to have its way and do what it chooses and pleases to do. However, you must obey God. You see, there is nothing wrong with you having fun and enjoying your youth. God does want you to have fun and enjoy your life however, this fun and enjoyment must be within the boundaries of God's Word and His standards as set out in His Word! The Word of God should be your final authority in every area of your life. God's Word demands total obedience and that's all that matters and that's all you should do. And like Paul put it:

Everything is permissible (allowable and lawful) for me; but not all things are helpful (good for me to do, expedient and profitable when considered with other things). Everything is lawful for me, but I will not become the slave of anything or be brought under its power. 1 Corinthians 6:12

Just because something is technically legal doesn't mean that it's spiritually appropriate. If I went around doing whatever I thought I could get by with, I'd be a slave to my whims. (The message)

"A young girl asked her friend if she could go on a picnic with her. She said to her friend, "wait just a minute, let me go and ask mother if it is OK." When she came back she told the other girl that her mother said she could not go. The other girl said to her, "you probably didn't talk hard enough. Don't let your mother go at that. God beg her some more and then she will probably let you go." She answered her friend by saying, "oh no, I would never do that. When my mother says 'no' she doesn't change her mind. She knows what is best for me, so I will do what she says."

Friend, that is the kind of attitude God desires for you to have toward Him and His Word and Will for your life; an absolute trust and obedience to Him, knowing that He loves you so dearly and knows the best for you, and wants you to have the best in life and be happy and safe.

You can make the choice today to begin to live a consistent life of obedience to God's Word. All you need is a willingness to do so. Willingness is when you don't feel like doing something but you decide to want to do it anyway. You cannot feel like reading the Word of God before you read it, you cannot feel like praying before you pray, you cannot feel like worshipping God before you do so, you cannot feel like going to church before you do so. You just have to do all of these because, its Gods will that you do them, and because Gods Word says you should.

Obedience requires action

Friend, you cannot feel like obeying God. You just have to obey God in spite of how you feel or think and in spite of your present situation. Tell me, do you wake up and FEEL black or white? You wake up and just know it. You just know that you are a black person or a white person. Remember, God has put greatness on the inside of you. You were created for signs and for wonders; you were created to succeed. If you want to live a life of success even as a teen, youth, young man or woman, you must live a consistent life of obedience to God, and to His Word!

You all probably know the story of Abraham and his son Isaac, and how God asked Abraham to go and sacrifice his only son Isaac to Him.

AFTER THESE events, God tested and proved Abraham and said to him, Abraham! And he said, here I am. [God] said, take now your son, your only son Isaac, whom you love, and go to the region of Moriah; and offer him there as a burnt offering upon one of the mountains of which I tell you. (Genesis 22:1-2)

Notice the Bible says TESTED, not TEMPTED Abraham, for God does not tempt us but He can and does test us. Now think about what would have happened if Abraham was disobedient to God in sacrificing his son in Genesis 22:1-14. What would history have recorded if he was disobedient? Friend, what has God asked you to do lately? Are you obedient to that last instruction God gave you? Have you ever thought about the fact that Isaac was also obedient to his father? Yes he was. This is because; he would have disobeyed his father to not be sacrificed.

He could probably have fought with his father not to bind him up for the sacrifice. However, he chose to stay calm and obeyed his father and allowed his father to bind him up and all of that for the sacrifice. God blessed Abraham because of his obedience to God. God was happy, delighted to know that He could trust Abraham. Isaac was also blessed with the promise God made to his father Abraham. (Genesis 26:2-5) Abraham's obedience not only affected his son's life and generation, it has also affected our generation. You and I can enjoy the blessings of Abraham too, because of His obedience to God. Your obedience will also affect others as much as it affects you. So also would your disobedience.

Friend, if God were to test your obedience, will you be found faithful? Or have you failed already? What choices are you making regarding being obedient? Abraham was faced with two choices – to obey God or to disobey God; to love his son above God or to love God above his son. Abraham didn't even give it a second thought; he chose to obey God straight away. He chose to love God above everything else, even above his only beloved son Isaac. Abraham chose to trust God, he knew in whom he had believed. He didn't know how God would do it, but he knew that God would not fail him. We ought to have such trust and confidence in God.

Do you love God only when things are working well for you? Do you obey God only when you are happy because all seems well for you? Or do you obey God seasonally? When a challenge comes to you, do you disobey God and choose to do things your own way instead of Gods way? Do you love God for who He is or for just the blessings He brings to your life?

You see, Abraham was after the God of the blessings, the Blesser. He loved God with all his heart, soul, mind and strength and for who God was and is. And that's how much God wants you and me to love

Him. However, Saul was after the blessings and not the God of the blessings. He wasn't interested in the Blesser! Obedience is going all the way with all of your heart to do what God says for you to do in His Word. God demands that you obey Him fully. He wants you to do whatever He has asked you to do in His Word not as you want, but as He wants and pleases.

Cursed be he who does the work of the Lord negligently [with slackness, deceitfully]; and cursed be he who keeps back his sword from blood [in executing judgment pronounced by the Lord]. Jeremiah 48:10

Obedience requires personal commitment

Are you seeking to please men or God? Are you seeking to please your friends and peers rather than God? Do you care and put more weight on other people's opinions than Gods opinions? When Saul sinned against God and admitted it, he wasn't as concerned about making it right with God as much as his honour by the people. He was more concerned about being accepted by the people than God; he was more concerned about doing things to please the people, and getting their approval than he was concerned about his relationship with God. Saul's decision to disobey God was at a great price, one that was unnecessary and worthless as it were.

Friend, this ought not to be so. God will not bend His standards because of you. You must understand the responsibility you have taken upon yourself to be called a Christian proclaiming to the world that you are a child of the Most High God. You must understand the responsibility of carrying His Name, for God places a great importance to His Holy Name! Friend, you must choose to please God and not man. What God says about you is more important to what men say about you. Disobedience comes with consequences and don't you ever forget that. Remember what we discussed regarding living a life of discipline in a previous chapter? Although our flesh hates and despises correction and discipline, we need to keep our flesh in subjection to our spirit so that we can walk in obedience before God. You need to live a life of discipline to walk in obedience.

There is severe discipline for him who forsakes God's way; and he who hates reproof will die [physically, morally, and spiritually]. Proverbs 15:10

Suffice to say that as much as you are able to repent, ask God to forgive you and receive His forgiveness, some act of disobedience come with consequences that must still take their toll on you. An example among so many would be such as, having sex outside a marriage relationship. Even though God has forgiven you, you may still get pregnant. Your repentance may not necessarily stop the pregnancy. In other words, even after repentance, consequences still follow. David after being told that God was angry with Him and was going to deal with him was quick to repent, but he still was told by God through the prophet Samuel that his child (with Uriah's wife) would die. 2 Samuel 12:15-19

Disobedience is always followed by consequences and the best way to avoid the consequences of disobedience is to remain obedient. Live a life of obedience! Be careful who you hang around with and I know we have touched on these in one of the chapters in this book. Be very careful! Your free choice will always result in consequences which may either be good or bad consequences.

"Now these things are examples (warnings and admonitions) for us not to desire or crave or covet or lust after evil and carnal things as they did." 1 Corinthians 10

Jesus is our perfect example of a life of obedience to God. The Word of God says concerning Him that,

"While he lived on earth, anticipating death, Jesus cried out in pain and wept in sorrow as he offered up priestly prayers to God. Because He honoured God, God answered Him. Though he was God's Son, He learned trusting – obedience by what He suffered, just as we do. Then, having arrived at the full stature of His maturity and having been announced by God as high priest in the order of Melchizedek, he became the source of eternal salvation to all who believingly obey him." 1 Peter 1:9 (the message)

Friend, God has a specific purpose for your life, which you can only come to know if and only if you choose to live a consistent life of obedience to God and His Word; always giving Him first place in your life, before anything and anyone else. Remember, the devil is the enemy of your soul, and his ultimate mission is to keep you from being fruitful, effective and walking in your purpose. However, he can never defeat you, if you completely yield yourself to the Lord in total obedience.

There are no limitations to how much God is able to bless you when you walk in obedience to His Word. Age is no barrier. Whether you are as old as Abraham was or as young as King Josiah was, the benefits of obeying God will flow into your life! Praise the Lord! Hallelujah! Amen! All of these are meaningless without obedience to God. True worship is obedience! Make a difference, be the difference and DARE TO SHINE!

"If someone claims, "I know him well!" but doesn't keep his commandments, he's obviously a liar. His life doesn't match his words. But the one who keeps God's Word is the person in whom we see God's mature love. This is the only way to be sure we're in God. Anyone who claims to be intimate with God ought to live the same kind of life Jesus lived." 1 John 2:5-6 (the message)

Rewards of living a life of obedience

We all love rewards and that's a good thing anyway. God is a God of rewards too and He uses rewards to motivate us. The Bible says that He rewards all those who diligently seek Him, who obey His command even His Word.

"But without faith it is impossible to please and be satisfactory to Him. For whoever would come near to God must [necessarily] believe that God exists and that He is the rewarder of those who earnestly and diligently seek Him [out]." Hebrews 11:6

Let's look at some of the rewards of living an obedient life.

1. When you are obedient, God will honour you with His Presence. Doors of opportunity will be opened to you and you will become a terror to the devil. John 14:21

2. When you live a life of obedience, God will honour you with the anointing of the oil of gladness. He will promote you, exalt you above your peers and make your name great. Psalm 45:7

3. Obedience to God will cause God to honour you with His beauty by setting you apart as His vessel for His holy use and make you a blessing to the world. 2 Timothy 2:21

4. When you live a life of obedience to God, God will honour your word and honour you with answered prayer. James 5:17-18

5. Obedience to God will cause God to honour you with victory over your enemies, with His blessings and your earthly inheritance. Deuteronomy 11

Remember:

- God requires for you to live a consistent life of obedience to Him. Obedience comes with rewards.
- The choice of obedience will lead you into a life of blessings and the choice of disobedience will lead you into a life of curses, problems and even death.
- Walking in obedience would require you to regularly study the Word and have daily fellowship with God.
- Living a life of obedience will protect you and cause the blessings of God to flow in your life
- Disobedience is always followed by consequences and the best way to avoid the consequences of disobedience is to remain obedient.
- If you resign yourself to partially obeying God, you will limit your spiritual growth and fail to receive all of the blessings and goodness of God for your life.

Think on these:

Obedience involves a willingness to always want to do what God says, in His Word. It is not dependent on how you feel, think, or what you see or what people say; but a willingness to do what the Word of God says, no matter what. It is doing the right thing no matter the pressure around you or on you.

Your thoughts:

Study Questions

1. What is obedience before God?

----

2. When you think of obedience can you truly say that you have been faithful?

----

3. Are you following your own ways, rather than following God's way?

----

4. Mention some of the reasons why you should live a life of obedience to God?

----

5. Is it something you think you cannot achieve and why?

Principle #10
It's Your Call – A final word!

Dear friend, now that you have read and gone through these life changing principles in this book, if you will put these into practice in your daily life, you will create a great future for yourself. God has a great plan and destiny for your life. However, this great plan can only become a reality if you are in Christ Jesus, if you are born again. That is the first step towards walking in that great plan and destiny. I want you to know that God loves you in spite of what you have done in your life, He loves you so much that He chose to die for you, so that you can have a good life in Him and be the best that He has called you to be. The Bible says in John 3:16

For God so greatly loved and dearly prized the world that He [even] gave up His only begotten (unique) Son, so that whoever believes in (trusts in, clings to, relies on) Him shall not perish (come to destruction, be lost) but have eternal (everlasting) life.

Jesus, the Son of the living God, laid down His precious life and rose again from the dead so that you would spend eternity with Him in Heaven and experience the very best, even His very best here on earth. The choice you make today, to receive Him into your heart and life as your Lord and Saviour will determine the course, quality and effectiveness of your life. Will you make that choice today and now? Remember your destiny comes not through chance but through choice. There is nothing more important than knowing God and having an intimate personal relationship with His Son Jesus Christ. It is the best decision you will ever make.

It is not enough to say you believe in God, it is not enough to go to church every now and then, it is not enough to hear or listen to good Bible messages, and it is not even enough to read the Bible. You must go the extra mile, take the next step and most important one that is, to make the choice to 'do' what the Bible says. Receive Jesus Christ into your life as your Lord and Saviour. Be born again.

Jesus answered him, I assure you, most solemnly I tell you, that unless a person is born again (anew, from above), he cannot ever see (know, be acquainted with, and experience) the Kingdom of God. John 3:3

God has an awesome plan and purpose for your life. He has this great destiny for you to accomplish but you cannot and will not be able to know His purpose for your life let alone fulfil it if you are not born again. Friend, true lasting success in life can only be achieved in Christ Jesus and nothing or no one else. He wants you to be happy, have and enjoy a good life, but this is only possible in Him.

For we are God's [own] handiwork (His workmanship), recreated in Christ Jesus, [born anew] that we may do those good works which God predestined (planned beforehand) for us [taking paths which He prepared ahead of time], that we should walk in them [living the good life which He prearranged and made ready for us to live]. Ephesians 2:10

However, you have to realise that you have a part to play in order to reach and fulfil this destiny and good life. God has called you to be a light even in the midst of darkness. He has called you to shine! Friend, God cares about you, more than you could or would ever imagine. I ask you right now to make the choice to accept Jesus into your life. The Bible says that if you acknowledge and confess with your lips that Jesus is Lord and in your heart believe, that God raised Him from the dead, you will be saved. For with the heart a person believes and so is justified, and with the mouth he confesses, declares openly and speaks out freely his faith and confirms his salvation. For who so ever shall call upon the Name of the Lord shall be saved. Make the choice to call on that Name right now.

Please pray this prayer with me, right now where you are and mean it from your heart.

Dear Lord, I come to you in the Name of Jesus. I admit that I am a sinner. I make the decision today to turn away from my sin and I ask you to forgive me and cleanse me from all unrighteousness. I ask you to come into my life and be my Lord and Saviour. I thank you for your Word that says in Acts 2:21 that, whosoever shall call on the Name of the Lord shall be saved. I call on you right now. I believe that you died on the cross for me, and I believe that God raised you up from the dead, according to Romans 10:9-10 that says that, if I shall confess with my mouth the Lord Jesus, and shall believe in my heart that God raised Him from the dead, that I shall be saved. With my heart I believe unto righteousness and with my mouth I confess unto salvation. Thank you for coming into my life as my Lord and Saviour, in Jesus Name, Amen.

Dear friend, if you have prayed this prayer from your heart, you are born again. I rejoice with you and heaven rejoices with you too! Make it a part of your daily routine to study and meditate on the Word of God. The Word of God will change your life and show you God's awesome plan and purpose for your life. Find a church that preaches the Word of God without compromise and join them. Share your faith with others. Your best days have just begun! God bless you.

Study the Word of God daily

1. The Word of God will nurture you and cause you to grow into maturity. 1 Peter 2:2.

2. The Word of God is your daily bread. It is your spiritual food. Just as you need food for your body, you need to also eat the food of God's Word for your spiritual growth. Matthew 4:4

3. The Word of God will give you wisdom, instruction and give you understanding for Salvation, which comes through faith in Christ Jesus. 2 Timothy 3:15. See also Psalm 119:99 and Proverbs 2:1-6

4. God's Word will guide you like a bright light on your path and protect you. Psalm 119:105, Proverbs 6:23. See also Psalm 91:11-12

5. Studying God's Word will bring you good success in life and in everything you do. It will bring about God's blessings into your life. Joshua 1:8; James 1:25. See also Psalms 1:1-3

6. Studying God's Word will equip you for good works. It will teach you how to live the way God has called you to live in Him and for Him and according to His Word; living a holy life and pleasing to God. 2 Timothy 3:16-17

7. Studying God's Word will bring joy, gladness and rejoicing into your life. Jeremiah 15:16

8. Studying God's Word will help you, and teach you how to resist temptation. Psalm 32:8, Psalm 119:9-11

Remember:

- Knowing Jesus as your Lord and Saviour is the first step to having true success in life.
- Making the decision to accept Jesus into your life is the best decision you would ever make in your life
- Daily studying the Word will reveal that plan and purpose to you
- The Word of God is your daily bread
- Make the choice today to be different, make a difference and DARE TO SHINE!

Think on these:

God created us to be a people who are capable of making the right choices. It is never too late to make the right choice. Remember, when you have made your choice, you have no power to choose the consequences.

Your thoughts:

Conclusion

Now that you have finally read through this book, it is my prayer that the life changing principles in this book would provide a clear understanding about the choices you make on a daily basis and the fact that every choice you make in life has a consequence; that this book would help you to begin to make the right choices that would change your life for the good.

Your guarantee to building a great future and discovering your destiny will be determined by the choices you make. However, these choices must be based on and line up with God's Word. I encourage you to begin today to make the right choices. God has a great plan for your life and He desires for you to be the best in life and have the best in Him, but this can only become a reality if you are making the right choices.

Evaluate yourself; evaluate your earnest desires and passions, your relationships, your daily routine and your habits. Are they lined up with God's Word? Friend, the choice is yours but choose today to begin a new life with these principles in operation in your everyday life. Spend time building an intimate relationship with God. Invest in your talents and gifts. Use it for the good of man and for the glory of God. Remain focused and don't allow anything or person to distract you. Shake away procrastination from your life. Make the choice to begin to do what you need to do and at the right time. Change your old habits and embrace the new, even with the principles outlined in this book. Take a step in faith, you can do it. The Principles in this book are simple and yet profound and can be achieved. It may seem difficult at first, but don't quit, soon you will have full control of your emotions. You can do all things in Christ Jesus.

As I come to the end of this book, I would like to reiterate the statement I made at the beginning of this book that says "Life is full of choices." I am personally challenged each day of my life with what

I have shared in this book. I determine each day to remain motivated and stay focused even when circumstances and people around me want me to quit. When I make mistakes, I repent immediately, receive God's forgiveness and pick up myself again and move on, choosing not to dwell on the past mistake. Each day, I try to be disciplined in acquiring information, reading and studying good life changing books. This is hard work but it pays off and is worth every bit of the effort put in. I remain positive even in the midst of every negative situation and believe in myself, daily speaking to the giant in me and affirming myself through God's Word.

I have discovered a deep sense of self worth and fulfilment that has given greater meaning and purpose to everything in my life. You too can experience this. You can be all that God has called you to be. Believe in yourself and believe in the ability that God has put in you and walk in it. God will never give up on you; I will not give up on you either, so please, do not give up on yourself. God loves you so dearly. I encourage you with all my heart to start today. You too can build a great future and discover your destiny. The choice is yours.

God bless you.

About the Author

Rosemary Okolo graduated from the University of Jos, Nigeria where she studied Law. She graduated from the Nigerian Law School, was called to the Nigerian Bar Association and practiced as a Solicitor. She has a Master of Law Degree (LLM) International Trade Law from the United Kingdom. She is an author, music minister and a song writer with a passion for God. Rosemary says, "My greatest desire is to be all that God has called me to be, to fulfil the purpose of God for my life and see people living and fulfilling their purpose in God especially young people." Rosemary has a passion to reach out to the world through music, writing books and ministering the Word. She is the author of Speak the Word in the face of your circumstances. Rosemary is happily married to husband Charles and they have three children, Sophia, Micaiah and Dorothy. They live in the United Kingdom.

NOTES

NOTES

NOTES

NOTES

NOTES